The Soul of Creative Writing

Books by Richard Goodman
French Dirt: The Story of a Garden in the South of France
The Soul of Creative Writing

The Soul of Creative Writing

Richard Goodman

Transaction Publishers
New Brunswick (U.S.A.) and London (U.K.)

Second paperback printing 2009

Copyright © 2008 by Transaction Publishers, New Brunswick, New Jersey.

"In Search of the Exact Word" first appeared in *The Oxford American Writer's Thesaurus*. "The Music of Prose" and "Using the Techniques of Fiction to Make Your Creative Nonfiction Even More Creative" first appeared in *The Writer's Chronicle*.

This book is printed on acid-free paper that meets the American National Standard for Permanence of Paper for Printed Library Materials.

Library of Congress Catalog Number: 2008001821
ISBN: 978-1-4128-0746-3 (cloth) 978-1-4128-1051-5 (paper)
Printed in the United States of America

Library of Congress Cataloging-in-Publication Data
Goodman, Richard, 1945-
  The soul of creative writing / Richard Goodman.
      p. cm.
  Includes bibliographical references and index.
  ISBN 978-1-4128-0746-3 (acid-free paper)
      1. English language—Rhetoric.   2. Creative writing.   I. Title.

PE1408.G6127 2008
808'.042—dc22   2008001821

To Brenda Bowen and Mary Downs
Hearts of gold

Contents

Acknowledgements

Without the help, care, and guidance of certain people, this book would not exist—or in any case it would be a much lesser book. I want to thank Sena Jeter Naslund and the MFA in Writing Program at Spalding University where some of these essays had their origins. I want to thank my trusted friend and unerring critic, Deborah Attoinese for her brilliance and generosity. I want to thank my erudite editor Larry Mintz, for all his help. I also want to thank John Taylor, Erin McKean, Roy Hoffman, Susan Tifft, Molly Peacock, Alex Jones, Robert Finch, Martha Goodman, Kenny Cook, Kaylene Johnson, and John Thornton. I want to especially thank Jo Boufford for her steadfast support through the years. I am most grateful to her. Though she shares the dedication of this book, I want to say here how much my sister, Mary Downs, has helped me through the years, in so many ways. I am lucky to have her as my sister. And I want to thank my beautiful, brilliant daughter, Becky, for all the light and love she brings to my life. Most of all I want to thank Rick Moranis. In countless discussions after our squash games, we talked about these essays. We also talked about them in e-mails, on the telephone, and in various walks around New York City. His insights, suggestions and comments were always incisive, smart, and inspiring. And correct. He has consistently been a great, generous advocate for this book, and I can't express my gratitude to him forcefully enough.

* * *

I have not included those eye-stopping numbers in the text to indicate the source for a quotation. The citations are in the Notes section at the end of the book, referenced by chapter and page number. While recognizing the need to cite my sources, I also want the experience for the reader to be as pleasurable as possible.

Introduction

I think all creative writers realize at a certain point that language will be the one friend and ally that will never desert them. There is a moment when writers know they won't be making the journey alone, that they will have a constant companion, and an astonishing one at that. Writers sit down at the desk with very little. It used to be a pen or pencil and some paper, or perhaps a typewriter. Now, many of us sit down to word processors. But, still, it's the most meager of work stations when the writer sits down to face the humbling blank page. Except that each time he or she does, language is there, too. It's the other welcome, steadfast companion in that silent room.

And what an ally it is. It's not just steadfast, but agile, muscular, resourceful, subtle, untiring. It's been fashioned by thousands of anonymous donors—men and women, scribes, rulers, soldiers, farmers, engineers, sailors, explorers, poets, bakers, preachers, hobos, weavers, singers, magicians—everyone and anyone who has ever grappled with expressing something and who has tried to articulate that concept or thing or action with, first, sounds and then, later, with written shapes.

Language is owned by no one. Language as it exists in the dictionary is a deep ocean of living words, as varied as undersea life, there for every one of us. Land can be owned—it can be sectioned, fenced off. Water can be owned—whole lakes, pretty and deep, are owned by individuals. Even the sky can be owned. In New York, and in other cities, "air rights," the space above a building, are sold for millions of dollars. Language, though, can't be owned. It can be corrupted, true, and it can be prostituted, and it can be regulated. But it cannot be owned. Each and every person in this country—and this is true of course with every language in every country—inherits the English language when he or she is born. It's an enormous, complex, inexhaustible gift.

This book, then, is an expression of gratitude for that gift. Each of these chapters is an attempt to illuminate the depth and subtlety, the muscularity, the grace of our language. It is a homily to its qualities.

1

Writers love words the way a yachtsman loves boats, the way a carpenter loves wood. Writers love *language*. Writers cannot be smarter than language, however. They can never totally master it. Even the greatest fall short. As T.S. Eliot wrote in "East Coker,"

> So here I am, in the middle way, having had twenty years—
> Twenty years largely wasted, the years of *l'entre deux guerres*—
> Trying to learn to use words, and every attempt
> Is a wholly new start, and a different kind of failure
> Because one has only learnt to get the better of words
> For the thing one no longer has to say, or the way in which
> One is no longer disposed to say it. And so each venture
> Is a new beginning, a raid on the inarticulate
> With shabby equipment always deteriorating
> In the general mess of imprecision of feeling,
> Undisciplined squads of emotion.

Billy Collins writes about poetry being the "result of a negotiation between the poet and an essentially uncooperative language." Faulkner spoke of *The Sound and the Fury* as his "best failure." The language is uncooperative like the sea is. It cannot be tamed by one writer, it is not meant to be tamed by anyone. Honest writers understand this relationship with their language, and are humbled by it. As a sailor must be humbled by the immense, unlimited power of the sea. Our efforts are imperfect, as they must be. But the challenge is forever compelling, and interesting. Our language forever inspires us, with its depth and beauty, to try again.

This book was written after a lifetime of working and struggling with words, of coming into intimate contact with the English language. Every day and every year, I have become more impressed with the bounty of our tongue. I continue to be astonished at what other writers can and have done with the language. Reading is more a less a tour of a writer's efforts at manipulating the language to create art, to create flesh and blood and mountains, cities, homes and gardens out of inky symbols on the page. The great pleasure of reading is experiencing how the most sensitive, inventive minds use language to create undiscovered countries, to create "imaginary gardens with real toads in them," as Marianne Moore described it. It's the heart's architecture fashioned by words, by language.

Why did I become a writer? I think I can trace the origins of the kind of writer I am to a few distinct sources. One of these is my mother. I didn't realize this until the end of her life when we would talk on the phone, she in Florida, I in New York. At one point my ear began to speak to me, to tell me, "How well she's using words! How interestingly! Listen to the sentences she's creating, how direct and precise they are. Listen to how she always chooses the right word." I realized that as a boy, this respect for, and facility with, words she had must have seeped into my body as surely as the Virginia air I breathed. She was my pre-Muse, without my knowing it.

Then there was the church, the small, red brick Virginia Episcopal church I attended—reluctantly. Those words and phrases I heard in church from the King James Bible were not like any other I ever heard. Nobody I knew ever said to me, "He maketh me to lie down in green pastures: he leadeth me beside the still waters." Nobody informed me that words could be arranged like that, made to express sounds like that. Nobody ever expressed an idea like, "Follow me, and I will make you fishers of men." But when I went to church, I heard this music, again and again. I didn't always understand a lot of what I heard. When the preacher said that a house divided against itself cannot stand, I didn't know what he meant, but my body responded to the music, and excited me somewhere between my heart and my soul.

Then there was the moment when as a boy of twelve I was reading *Robinson Crusoe,* and I saw Friday's footprints in the sand. There was someone else on that island! You—Robinson Crusoe—won't be alone anymore! I somehow knew after that words, mere words, could make me feel great emotions. Words written in a book by a man from another country and long dead could make my heart skip two beats. I learned that any book I picked up might do wonderful things. Somewhere inside me I wanted to possess that magic.

There were all these things, and more—libraries, teachers, an award or two, and even the dictionary. The dictionary. It was the key to the kingdom, the kingdom of words where I wanted to reside.

Ever since men and women began putting pen to paper, or bytes to screen, they have struggled with this untamable ocean that is our language. Writers have grappled with the same problems, with the same "general mess of imprecision of feeling," T.S. Eliot spoke of, bemoaned the same shortcomings of theirs, achieved some well-earned victories and similar defeats in trying to describe, as Faulkner put it, "the problems of the human heart in conflict with itself." Faulkner spent a lifetime "in the agony and sweat of the human spirit," wrestling with the great English language, just as all writers have, still do, and will do. Writers are linked to the writers of the past, great and small, because of this. This is what we do. It is a privilege, both humbling and endlessly inspiring, to work daily, "trying to hit the head on the nail," as John Berryman wrote, with this magnificence that is English.

This book is a testament to that struggle.

Part 1

Words

1

The Music of Prose

"Stories do not give instruction, they do not explain how to love a companion or how to find God. They offer, instead, patterns of sound and association, of event and image."—Barry Lopez, About This Life: Journeys on the Threshold of Memory

Language is sound by which we communicate. You could say it's organized sound. Or patterned sound. Or sound charged with meaning. But it's still sound. You listen to me speak, and you're listening to sound. But it's variable sound. It's sound with—pauses. With *emp*hasis. With, well, you know, a certain rhythm.

In writing, the kind of sound the writer makes on the page is crucial to our liking his or her prose, or not. When we read prose, we hear it. As Eudora Welty wrote in *One Writer's Beginnings*, "Ever since I was first read to, then started reading to myself, there has never been a line read that I didn't *hear.* As my eyes followed the sentence, a voice was saying it silently to me." How prose writers are different is, among other things, the sound they make on the page. The sound of Raymond Carver on the page is very different from the sound Henry James makes on the page. A sentence is far more than information.

In another way of speaking about this, Jean Cocteau said he knew Shakespeare was a great writer, even without Cocteau's knowing a single word of English. He could hear it in the sounds the words made.

At the highest level, the sound a writer makes on the page is music.

So you can say writing is music we can all read. Instead of clef notes, sharps and minors, full stops or half stops, and all the other symbols actual music employs, English has letters, syllables, and words. It has many methods by which to control the sounds it produces. Some of these methods are subtle and require great practice to use them expertly, like playing an instrument well requires dedicated practice. What order the words are placed in the sentence can determine what kind of sound, or

7

melody, emerges. However, that sentence will not stand alone and must be taken in context with others sentences, so its individual music may be sublimated to the larger melody of the paragraph. Punctuation is another determiner of what kind of sound the sentence makes and how it makes it. For example, I can. Make. You. Read. At. The. Pace. That. I. Want. You. To. Simply. By. This. Little. Dot.

In fact, the English language is an enormous musical instrument. It's made up of words which are in turn made of syllables that are stressed or unstressed. So right there we have a basis for music—dissimilarity. It is this simple concept—stressed and unstressed syllables—that is at the heart of it all. The words, and stresses, are placed in combinations and orders that produce a kind of melody. Think of the famous opening to Beethoven's Fifth Symphony: Dah dah dah *dah.* So much of the drama comes from the simple idea of the last note's heavy stress. Despite what Molière had his bourgeois gentleman say, we actually speak quite often in poetry—in iambics, or in blank verse. Or in some version of stressed/unstressed syllabism. The music of prose has, in its own way, the variety, scope, shadings, colors, melodies, and drama of music that is played on instruments.

Why are we concerned with music in writing at all? Because *we* are musical. We are essentially musical, we humans. We are musical for the simple, profound reason that we have a heart. From the moment we're born—no, actually, before we're born—we have a steady, consistent, basic beat of our heart inside us: ba-*bump* ba-*bump*. Our blood surges and retreats, like a tide. So inside us we have an unstressed and stressed beat, the basis for music, a pulse. I believe that's one reason why we respond to music and seek to create it. It comes naturally, by way of our own body.

The two main elements of prose are music and meaning. It's a little artificial to talk about the music of prose without talking about meaning, as well. It's a bit like talking about the melody of a song without its lyrics. That's really half a song. In reality, the prose writer's task is to balance the two, and that balance may be equal or unequal, depending on the desired effect and on the relationship with other words and sentences. Sometimes music takes a back seat to meaning, sometimes meaning has to move over for music. That's one reason why a good writer has to have a good ear.

Cleanth Brooks asked Robert Frost about music in writing and its origins:

"Would you say that even though the meter is based on the human pulse or some kind of basic rhythm in our natures…it's something to be fought with, to be tussled with? It's not directly expressive—ta-DA, ta-DA, ta-DA, ta-DA, ta-DA."

Frost replied, "No, it's doggerel when you do that. You see, and how you save it from doggerel is having enough dramatic meaning in it for the other thing to break the doggerel."

Good prose is musical. Like actual music, it can be lyrical, tender, and soft. It can be dissonant, harsh, blunt. It can be grand. It can be simple. It can be comic or tragic. It employs many of the same methods as actual music: rhythm, harmony, counterpoint, and balance. It can produce sounds that, at the highest level, have a unique melody. Take the beginning to Charles Dickens' *A Tale of Two Cities*, "It was the best of times, it was the worst of times." Why is that sentence remembered by practically anyone who reads it? It's not because of the content. It's because of the *music*. Every fine writer produces a kind of music with his or her writing. It's also called style. A great writer will almost have us humming the melody he or she makes on the page. Great writers are great composers.

We know about the music of poetry. Poetry is supposed to be musical. So, we want it to be read aloud, the better to catch its brilliant rhythms and melodies, its cadence, its beat. The writer sings his or her creation, in a way. I did read recently about a poet who said reading aloud robs readers of the ability to make their own decisions about how and when to place stress and emphasis on the words in the poem. But you can have both, can't you? You can read the poem yourself. When we hear a poem, we better understand that often the sound *is* the meaning, or that sound and meaning together are what makes it poetry. When we hear "Shall I compare thee to a summer's day? / Thou art more lovely and more temperate," can we really distinguish between sound and meaning?

We seldom think of prose in this way. But the music of prose is one of the things that makes it unique and pleasurable. Some writers refer to this as the style of a writer—E. B. White, for one. Here's what he said in *The Elements of Style*: "When we speak of Fitzgerald's style, we don't mean his command of the relative pronoun, we mean the sound his words make on the paper." But you can see White chose to describe the phenomenon of style with the musical word *sound.* So what others may call style, I—and others—call music. Here's what Susan Cheever once said in an interview: "When you write, you're creating music inside the reader's head. One of the many important things about music is rhythm, and that's sentence structure. If you're not paying attention to sentence structure, it's like you're playing notes without rhythm. How crazy would that be? You must pay attention to the rhythm of your sentences and the rhythm of your words—each word has a rhythm. You should be scanning your lines even in nonfiction prose."

One of the best ways of looking at the idea of rhythm and music in prose is to write the same thing in three or four different ways. That is, to experiment with a concept in which all the variations say what needs to be said and the differences are matters of rhythm and melody.

So, for example, let's turn to murder. Here are four ways of telling the reader you shot a woman:

I picked up the gun and shot her.
I picked up the gun, and I shot her.
I picked up the gun. I shot her.
I picked up the gun. Then I shot her.

Each of these sentences provides the reader with all the information about the killing he or she needs. But you can provide the reader with various melodies with each of these choices, and each one is slightly different. (I won't even go into different verbs—e.g., I picked up the gun and I killed her.) So, if each of these sentences packs the same information, on what do you base your choice? On music. Of course, as was mentioned, the music in writing is never isolated. But that's another matter. Something in the melody will appeal to you more in one of these sentences, and you'll choose it. When you do make your choice, you usually have a sense of regret, because the other versions possess qualities you wish your choice had, but you can't have everything. Writers live with that.

As Thomas Pynchon wrote, "Writers are naturally drawn, chimpanzee-like, to the color and the music of this English idiom we are blessed to have inherited. When given the choice we will usually try to use the more vivid and tuneful among its words."

A deft use of punctuation can produce lyrical writing. Take the comma. Just look at this masterful use of commas from Mark Twain. This passage is from *Huckleberry Finn*. Huck's way down the river at this point, and he comes ashore and sees a circus:

It was a real bully circus. It was the splendidest sight that ever was, when they all come riding in, two and two, a gentleman and lady, side by side, the men just in their drawers and under-shorts, and no shoes or stirrups, and resting their hands on their thighs, easy and comfortable—there must a' been twenty of them—and every lady with a lovely complexion, and perfectly beautiful, and looking just like a gang of real sure-enough queens, and dressed in clothes that cost millions of dollars, and just littered with diamonds. It was a powerful fine sight; I never see anything so lovely. And then one by one they got up and stood, and went a-weaving around the ring so gentle and wavy and graceful, the men looking ever so tall and airy and straight, with their heads bobbing and skimming along, away up there under the tent-roof, and every lady's rose-leafy dress flapping soft and silky around her hips, and she looking like the most loveliest parasol.

No wonder Faulkner said he had to wait five years each time before he reread *Huckleberry Finn.* With his commas precisely placed to produce a cadence like the gait of a horse, Twain guides and controls our eye. The writing isn't excited or exclamatory; it's calm and easy, letting the element of wonder, such a delicate thing, take precedence in our mind. Twain also uses the word "and" to keep the writing connected and all of one steady pace, even as he breaks it into an easy rhythm with those commas. Hemingway learned a lot from Twain. A great writer will have such control over his or her composition that he or she will force you, the reader, to read it—and hear it—precisely the way he or she wants you to. Twain does just that here.

Comedic writing, which may, at first, seem far from musical, is, in fact, the most musical of writing in many ways. What is comedy but the perfect use of caesura? What's the difference between: "Take my wife, please," and "Take my wife. Please." *Everything.* Yet the difference is a single musical note, or, rather, beat. These are exactly the same words, but the reactions couldn't be more different. Comedic writing relies on musical choices. A great comedic writer must have a great ear.

Music in prose isn't always mellifluous. That's because the music really never stands alone. If the story is austere, the music can be, too. You can see this plainly in detective stories. You may call this crime writing or murder mysteries or whatever. But at its best, it's just plain fine writing. Period. I love the music of good detective fiction. Because it's about crime and punishment, you're going to get the kind of prose that reflects the people who deal with that world. Here's the beginning of *The Postman Always Rings Twice*, by James M. Cain:

They threw me off the hay truck about noon. I had swung on the night before, down at the border, and as soon as I got up there under the canvas, I went to sleep. I needed plenty of that, after three weeks in Tia Juana, and I was still getting it when they pulled off to one side to let the engine cool. Then they saw a foot sticking out and threw me off.

This is music without flourish, without trills. Not an extra note anywhere. That's the way it is throughout the lean 116-page novel. Ever notice how taut and brief so much detective fiction is? Not a single adjective or adverb here. Why this kind of writing is so terribly difficult to do is that the nouns and verbs carry the tune, and you had better be very attuned to your character and your story or the whole thing will fall apart.

Now, compare James M. Cain's beginning to the beginning of William Faulkner's story, "Barn Burning":

The store in which the Justice of the Peace's court was sitting smelled of cheese. The boy, crouched on his nail keg at the back of the crowded room, knew he smelled cheese, and more: from where he sat he could see the ranked shelves close-packed with the solid, squat, dynamic shapes of tin cans whose labels his stomach read, not from the lettering which meant nothing to his mind but from the scarlet devils and the silver curve of fish—this, the cheese which he knew he smelled and the hermetic meat which his intestines believed he smelled coming in intermittent gusts momentary and brief between the other constant one, the smell and sense just a little of fear because mostly of despair and grief, the old fierce pull of blood.

Here, the unusual sequences are mirroring the boy's thought process, and yet it produces a unique music as well, so Faulkner has achieved the great Flaubertian balance between the meaning and the music of words. Faulkner always had sufficient dramatic meaning and worked incredibly hard to insure that when he broke with the heartbeat, the ta-Da, ta-DA, he did so with profoundly memorable song.

The introduction of detective fiction is a good place in which to talk about a change of *key*. We know how the shift from a major to a minor key in music can affect us, often with a sense of foreboding or melancholy. It can happen in prose, too. Take the start of James Crumley's first-rate book, *Dancing Bear*. Crumley begins his 228-page novel with a simple, easy sentence:

We had been blessed with a long, easy fall for western Montana.

It's lyrical and short, ending with that sing-y word, *Montana*. Then Crumley expands a bit, but still maintains his easy lyricism:

Two light snowfalls had melted before noon, and in November we had three weeks of Indian Summer so warm and seductive that even we natives seemed to forget about winter.

But what next? Darkness and drama, and a clear change of key, beginning with a hard conjunction:

> But in the canyon of Hell Roaring Creek, where I live, when the morning breezes stirred off the stone-cold water and into the golden dying rustle of the cottonwoods and creek willows, you could smell the sear, frozen heart of winter, February, or, as the Indians sometimes called it, the Moon of the Children Weeping in the Lodges, crying in hunger.

The information here isn't what sends a warning chill through your body. It's the foreboding music. Phrases of fear broken by commas: The word "Hell" affixed to the narrator's home; morning breezes "stirred"—a word associated with ghost and spirits; "off the stone-cold water"—we are no longer in the world of "warm and seductive"; and then those dreadful words, "dying, sear, frozen, Weeping, crying, hunger."

We are fairly certain we are not going to be treated to a pleasant book about the changes of seasons in Montana. Crumley's cold notes enter the bloodstream, and we know something is afoot.

I love the unique dissonance of Marianne Moore's prose. This is the arresting beginning to the "Foreword" from *A Marianne Moore Reader*:

> Published: it is enough. The magazine was discontinued. The edition was too small. One paragraph needs restating. Newspaper cuts on the fold or disintegrates. When was it published, and where? 'The title was "Words and..." something else. Could you say what it was?' I have forgotten.

Music is often about counterpoint. In writing, dialogue is all about counterpoint. When you discuss dialogue in American prose, you eventually will arrive at Hemingway's door. At his best, as in stories like "A Clean, Well-Lighted Place," he pumps the heart of the story by the crisp, cold dialogue of the two waiters hoping an old drunk sad man will leave the café so they can go home. The dialogue is almost like a call-and-answer chant. Whether they admit it or not, so many writers have drunk from Hemingway's spring. A story like "The Sea Change," with its relentlessly moving yet delicately balanced point-counterpoint, is still being written today. It begins:

> "All right," said the man. "What about it?"
> "No," said the girl. "I can't."
> "You mean you won't."
> "I can't," said the girl. "That's all that I mean."
> "You mean that you won't."
> "All right," said the girl. "You have it your own way."
> "I don't have it my own way. I wish to God I did."
> "You did for a long time," the girl said.

The dialogue goes on to reveal that the girl has had an affair with another woman. She says,

> "It doesn't do any good to say I'm sorry?"
> "No."
> "Nor to tell you how it is?"
> "I'd rather not hear."
> "I love you very much."
> "Yes, this proves it."
> "I'm sorry," she said, "if you don't understand."
> "I understand. That's the trouble. I understand."

What a bitter tune the two of them play, back and forth, one taking off from the other, as if it were a deadly jazz riff.

We get our doses of music in writing in unexpected ways sometimes. In government writing, for example. No, we don't find it in our tax forms, but in two of our most famous American documents, the Declaration of Independence and the Gettysburg Address. We may have seen the poetry in Lincoln's speech before, but what about Jefferson's composition? We've been exposed to this writing for as long as we can remember. We all know how it begins, "When in the course of human events…." And we also know so well the part that goes, "All men are created equal. They are endowed by their creator with certain unalienable rights. Among these are life, liberty and the pursuit of happiness." The word *unalienable,* so hard for children to pronounce, and with a meaning that is hard for a child to fathom, is nevertheless such a pretty sound. It takes six syllables to make that sound, so you don't leave that concept easily.

Jefferson was a great lover of music, and I believe that one reason he chose that word on that hot summer day in Philadelphia was for its music. Now, what's interesting is that Jefferson had originally written "We hold these truths to be self-evident: that all men are created equal; that they are endowed by their creator with inherent and inalienable rights." It was Congress who made Jefferson take out "inherent," thus depriving him of a nifty alliteration. They also, as you may notice, made him add the word "certain" before "inalienable." Even Jefferson had to get his work vetted and approved.

By the way, what's also interesting is that in his *Autobiography*, Jefferson has the word as *inalienable* in his version of the Declaration. How, I wonder, did it get switched to *unalienable*?

So, there is more music around us in the writing we are exposed to than we may think. Jefferson was deeply educated in English literature as well as in Greek and Latin literature. Who knows what caused him in the end to write "When in the course of human events"? I suspect that his rhythms in English derived in no small measure from Latin, as well as from English. Then a phrase kept slipping into my head, and finally made itself known, "Nel mezzo del cammin di nostra vita…" In the middle of the path of our life. The beginning of Dante's *Inferno*. The rhythm is similar to the beginning of the Declaration, and so is the meaning. I checked with Monticello, and they confirmed that Jefferson did indeed possess a copy of the *Divine Comedy* in Italian. So we do know at least that this poem was at part of Jefferson's verbal musical heritage and that he may have drawn upon it.

Music in writing is more than what happens in a single sentence. It's how that sentence performs in balance with the sentences that precede it and follow it. You may change or even eliminate a word or sentence because it's out of tune with its neighbors. So, as a writer, comedic or not, you have to develop a good ear. If you're lucky, you come from the South, where its entire history is an opera and every conversation is an aria. You will also be lucky as a Southerner in that your writing will inevitably be influenced by the speech of African Americans, people traditionally close to the land. The land informs and nurtures speech, as much as anything. But you will find inspiration in the music of the speech around you, wherever that is.

How do you become a better composer? Well, by writing, of course. Just as important, you need to be a desperate reader. Read everything that appeals to you, regardless of so-called merit. It has merit if you want to read it. This way, you'll be absorbing the music, the different styles, and you'll become aware of the vast possibilities. One critic speaking of the late Harold Brodkey's writing said that as a young man first reading Brodkey his reaction was, "You mean you can actually write sentences like that?" In the end we are all working to compose original music. None of us can do this without absorbing the great music of the great writers of the past.

It is often in the revision that we find the true melody and harmony of our writing. That's because these things are often a matter of subtle balances and intonations. We may not get it right on the first try. At a certain point as a writer you'll be attuned to whether or not your writing is on key or off key. I think it would be wonderful to hear a great writer explain why he or she felt the melody in a sentence or paragraph of his or hers was wrong. Then, right.

In the end, the creation of original music in prose—or style, if you will—is that mysterious combination of everything you've learned, read and practiced with who you are. It's unique, like your handwriting or fingerprint, though achieved with blood, sweat, and tears. But worth it. Because, in the end, as Flaubert said, "One must sing with one's own voice."

As I said, the music of great writers can be as complex and difficult to describe as actual music. Like any music by a great composer you love, you can eventually come to identify it, though you may not be able to describe how. Eventually, you are able to identify what is Hemingway, what is Henry James, what is Faulkner. As your ear gets better, you will also be able to recognize echoes of other writers' music in a writer's prose. If you listen closely, you can hear the melodies of Ring Lardner and F. Scott Fitzgerald in J.D. Salinger's prose just as surely as you can hear Mozart in early Beethoven. Sometimes the task is to escape the tunes of those who precede you, because their influence is so powerful. I always felt that being a writer in Mississippi with Faulkner looming over you was a bit like being Frank Sinatra, Jr. But Brad Watson has done just fine.

Sometimes, as with Gerard Manley Hopkins, a writer will compose in such as way as to override those natural stresses and create new ones, resulting in an original melody. But Hopkins, a poet, was forced to actually employ stress marks to show us what he was trying to do, because our inclination is to go with the norm. Robert Frost found this painful ("It is painful to watch our sprung-rhythmists straining at the point of omitting one short from a foot for relief from monotony"). Yet such was Hopkins' great power that one could say he succeeded far more often than not.

The attempts to set the work of writers to music America often seem unnecessary to me. Take Samuel Barber's setting of James Agee's "Knoxville: Summer 1915." Agee may have been our most conscious composer. He was *always* composing music, and in fact you can often sense his effort to create great music, and it can be distracting. In art, the effort should never be visible. But he hits all the right notes in "Knoxville: Summer 1915":

> On the rough wet grass of the back yard my father and mother have spread quilts. We all lie there, my mother, my father, my uncle, my aunt, and I too am lying there. First we were sitting up, then one of us lay down, and then we all lay down, on our stomachs, or on our sides, or on our backs, and they have kept on talking. They are not talking much, and the talk is quiet, of nothing in particular, of nothing at all in particular, of nothing at all.

What does that last sentence accomplish? Surely, it's not just a matter of conveying information to the reader, is it? Agee is lulling us with his music, lulling us into a state of dreaminess, so we can actually be with him on that summer evening. Barber's rendition of this is lyrical enough, but I submit that setting Agee's prose to music is gilding the lily. (Yeats told Robert Frost that there was "nothing he hated more than having his poems set to music.... It wasn't the tune he had in his ear.") I can see why Barber was drawn to Agee's prose as a composer, though.

The music of a book or story or essay can be a stronger or lesser element in it depending on the writer's predilections and talents. But the music is always there, even if it can only be faintly heard. The music of writing you encounter in books can be varied and different, and you may not like all of it. Probably not all of it, in fact. In the end it is often the music of the writing that turns you off, not what the writer is saying. You may grow out of it, too. I think one of the reasons I can no longer read Thomas Wolfe is that I no longer care for his music. I've grown out of it. Those long, sighing, longing sentences. Just as while I once thought *Bolero* was the greatest thing ever written, I'm not sure I could listen to it all the way through anymore. That's not true for Mozart's Haydn quartets, though, or for the Beatles' music. Or for Faulkner's short stories. Just so, you may not be prepared to listen to certain writer's music until you have reached a certain age.

I think it's also important to point out that a writer's music will change, develop and mature throughout his or her career. James Joyce provides no better example. In the beginning, we have the somber, simple rhythms of *Dubliners*. This is followed by a new freedom in *A Portrait of the Artist as a Young Man* that is exhilarating. In the end, we have *Finnegans Wake*, which you can say is one great huge Irish song that seems to have no confines whatsoever. Which do you prefer? You may be like the traditionalist Evelyn Waugh, who said Joyce started out fine enough with *Dubliners*, but then, basically, went mad. Or you may be like W. H. Auden, who liked the music of *Finnegans Wake* very much.

You will respond to music in your writing because of your body and your ear, but you must also work at it, too, as a composer of actual music must. You work at it as much with your ear as you do with your eye, though in time the two become, to borrow once more from Robert Frost, like your two eyes making one picture in sight. I think writing should be pleasing to the eye, but more pleasing to the ear. When we read, as Eudora Welty said, we hear the words, don't we? We may have stopped mouthing the words as we read long ago, but that doesn't stop our inner ear from listening. I think when we read we are more listening, in the end, than seeing. To be conscious of the music in your writing is merely an acknowledgement of how we read, of how we absorb words.

The novelist Robert Stone, author of *Dog Soldiers* and *Damascus Gate,* got into a bit of a pickle some years back over his novel, *Outerbridge Reach.* He was accused by an English writer of stealing facts from a nonfiction book the man had written and using them in his novel without proper acknowledgement. Stone wrote a letter of rebuttal in which he said that, well, I probably should have expressed my debt a bit more emphatically to your book, but that isn't the point. What's important, he said, is that I supplied the music.

2

In Search of the Exact Word

The exact word. *Le mot juste*, in French, is how it's expressed. *Mot* meaning "word," and *juste* meaning "exact." Most everyone I've ever talked to, or have read, attributes this phrase to Gustave Flaubert, the celebrated nineteenth-century French perfectionist author of *Madame Bovary* and *Sentimental Education*. Sven Birkerts, for example, wrote this in the *American Scholar,* "Like many would-be writers, I had been deeply influenced by stories of Flaubert's grail-quest for *le mot juste,* the exact word, which of course translated into the idea of the perfect sentence, paragraph, chapter...book." I've read the two-volume edition of Flaubert's letters, translated so wonderfully by Francis Steegmuller, at least seven or eight times, and I couldn't find the phrase. So I went to the web. I found "Le Mot Juste" Translation Service, "Le Mot Juste Communications," an e-zine named "Le Mot Juste," and an on-line dictionary with that name. I'm surprised I didn't find "Le Mot Juste" Escort Service.

There were lots of references to Flaubert and to *le mot juste*, but none told me *where* to find it. I finally did find what I wanted in a book in French by Charles Carlut, *La Correspondance de Flaubert; étude et répertoire critique*. It's an inventory of topics in Flaubert's letters with, God be praised, an excellent index. (It should be noted that Steegmuller did not translate all of Flaubert's letters.) I found Flaubert uses the expression just twice. He writes the critic Sainte-Beuve, "If I put "blue" after "stones," it's because "blue" is *le mot juste*, believe me." In the other instance, he says there has to be a rapport between *le mot juste* and *le mot musical*, that is, between the meaning and the music of a word. That's it, at least as far as I can determine. (I have since read somewhere that Flaubert makes other references to *le mot juste*—or to *le seul mot juste,* "the one and only right word"—but I haven't located them yet.)

Flaubert also uses the expression, *le mot propre*, "the proper word." That didn't seem to catch on.

Flaubert does say, though, that, "all talent for writing consists after all of nothing more than choosing words. It's precision that gives writing power." He also says that, "perfection has everywhere the same characteristic: that's precision, exactness." He says he spends hours looking for a word. He expressed the struggle this way: "I am the obscure and patient pearl-fisher, who dives deep and comes up empty-handed and blue in the face." And at another point, he writes a friend that he spent three days making two corrections and five days writing one page. Practically anything Flaubert says about writing and art is interesting, even if you disagree with him, though you are constantly reminded, as Henry James points out, that "he felt of his vocation almost nothing but the difficulty."

However many times he actually says *le mot juste*, Flaubert represents the relentless search for artistic perfection, whatever the issue. Ernest Hemingway—who admired Flaubert's discipline—actually uses the phrase "the exact word." He called Flaubert "our most respected, honored master." In his memoir about Paris, *A Moveable Feast,* Hemingway talks about Ezra Pound, saying, "here was the man I liked and trusted the most as a critic then, the man who believed in the *mot juste*—the one and only correct word to use—the man who had taught me to distrust adjectives as I would later learn to distrust certain people in certain situations...." Hemingway was profoundly good at finding the exact word. It's all there for you to see, this learning, in Hemingway's writing. "This was a man to whom words mattered," Joan Didion wrote. "He worked at them, he understood them, he got inside them." I'm a huge Hemingway fan just for his deep understanding of words alone.

Mark Twain was memorably good at seizing the exact word, too. Most humorists are. (Had Twain read Flaubert? I don't know. I would love to hear from a Twain scholar on this.) Their humor often depends on a choice of word; in fact the whole laugh can rest on a single word choice. When someone interviewed Evelyn Waugh for the *Paris Review,* they asked him about the process of creating a character. He said, "I regard writing not as an investigation of character, but as an exercise in the use of language." If you read the books of the comic writers just with this idea in mind—S. J. Perelman, Thurber, Twain, Waugh, even Woody Allen—you'll see how often the laugh comes from a single, well-chosen word placed exactly where it's liable to generate the loudest laugh. Of course, Twain wrote perhaps the most famous line about this particular topic ever written, "The difference between any word and the 'right' word is the difference between the lightning bug and the lightning."

Writers don't normally lack for reasons to be depressed or jealous, but in case you get low on fuel one day, think of this. Three of the best at this *mot juste* game did not speak or write English as their mother tongue. I mean Joseph Conrad, Isak Dinesen—I will draw on her work later in this chapter—and Vladimir Nabokov. For Conrad, who grew up speaking Polish, it wasn't even his *second* language, French was. Isak Dinesen's first language was Danish, Nabokov's Russian.

What *is* the exact word? I think what we usually mean by that is a word that not only conveys precisely what you, the writer, want to say, but also does it in an unforgettable way, a dramatic way, either because of its juxtaposition to its surrounding words or because it's employed in a fresh way, or both. Something else, too, I think: when it surprises, it's usually a surprise that's doesn't come out of a vacuum. It communicates resoundingly, because somewhere the reader understands the word well enough to appreciate its use.

So many things go into a writer's selection of a word. It's impossible to break it all down precisely, because the reasons and influences of your choices come from years of reading and assimilating other authors' choices and reveling in their surprises and delights. But maybe we can talk about a few of them. Each will have a different weight, depending on the circumstances. There's meaning, of course. The word has to mean what it is you want to say. Flaubert repeatedly says that if you really know what it is you want to say, then you'll find the right word. But what *is* meaning? Is it the dictionary meaning? Obviously, you can't use "blue" if you mean "red." That sounds pretty elementary, but believe me, I've put down words that *don't* mean what I *thought* they meant. It was only after I looked them up that I realized I was wrong. Take the word *livid*. What do you think it means? Now, look it up. Please get back to me with your results.

But isn't meaning more complex? Doesn't it include music, drama and mood? Doesn't it include physical appearance? Doesn't it include surprise and context? Otherwise, why choose "crimson" over "red?" Or "furious" over "angry?" There are shades of differences in their meanings, to be sure, but there are other more prominent differences between these words. Not only does "crimson" sound different than "red,"—and we do "hear" words when we read them, don't we?—it *looks* different.

How a word looks on the page can be important; it can be pleasing or annoying. That's part of its meaning, isn't it?

I would say it includes something else, something as important if not more so—the "secret strength" of the word, as Milan Kundera expressed it. (More on this later.) By that, he means its roots and derivation, its history. I couldn't agree more. Which is why I dote on the dictionary and lean on it like a cane as I go hobbling through my process of composition. I love the dictionary—not every single dictionary, but those at the top of the lexicographic ladder: *Webster's Third International*, *Random House Unabridged, American Heritage Dictionary* and, of course, the vast *Oxford English Dictionary*, the *OED*. These are fat books—in the *OED's* case, truly overweight—devoted entirely to single words. There are no favorites in the dictionary; it's the ultimate non-discriminatory book. At least, mostly. That's why you can have "slut" right next to "slushy," "barfly" just before "bargain," and "steal" on the tail of "steak set." True, the dictionary has taken more to using epithets such as "obscene," "pejorative," and "offensive," but in the end these apply to very few words, and I for one don't always agree with the dictionary's opinions and often ignore them. More on the dictionary later.

That's a lot to consider. But the fact is, some choices take more thinking about than others. Some thinking takes longer than other thinking with regards the selection of a word. You can spend ten seconds choosing a word or twenty minutes—or days, if you're as driven as M. Flaubert. And everything in between and beyond. The thing is, though, there are many pains in writing, but one of its most narcotic joys is putting down a word you believe does the job extraordinarily well. It's just *right*. It's *juste*. When you see it there, on the page, grinning out at you in all its handsome self, you know it's been worth the effort. And when you return to it, it will still be just as handsome.

I'd like to cite a few examples.

One thing about words is that some of them have developed an association specific to one gender. Words such as "pretty," "giggly," "flirtatious." If you did an informal poll and asked, for example, what gender do you think of—*quick*—when you hear the word "pretty," what would it be? By the same token, if you took the words "crude," "killer," and "ravenous," what gender would spring to mind? The thing is, though, these words inherently *don't* belong to any gender. I think a writer should always keep his or her peripheral vision attuned to use one of these pigeonholed words for the unexpected gender, sort of like cross-dressing when you're writing. Boswell, in his life of Samuel Johnson, describes a scene in which Johnson berates a poor servant girl: "You blockhead!" Dr. Johnson says. Boswell, in an aside, says that at first he thought it strange to call a *woman* a blockhead but, after thinking about it, there was really no reason why you shouldn't. This role reversal in one reason why the name "Pretty Boy Floyd" is so memorable. It's also one of the reasons the word "handsome" catches the eye when applied to a woman. And so on.

Another area that has not nearly been mined comes from the definitions of the words themselves. In an essay about—who else?—Samuel Johnson, T. S. Eliot wrote, "Nowadays we use words so loosely that a writer's meaning may sometimes be concealed from us, simply because he has said exactly what he meant." In my experience, this usually means the writer is using the word in its original sense, or its first meaning in the dictionary. In *A Moveable Feast*, Hemingway describes eating some oysters in a café:

> I began my second dozen of the flat oysters, picking them from their bed of crushed ice on the silver plate, watching their unbelievably delicate brown edges react and cringe as I squeezed lemon juice on them and separated the holding muscle from the shell and lifted them to chew them carefully.

The edges *cringed*. We associate that word now mainly with fear, but that's not it's first meaning, which is, "to draw in or contract one's muscles involuntarily." The word comes from the Old English *cringan,* "to fall, yield." It's not that we don't understand Hemingway, it's that we might be taken slightly aback. What do you mean—that the oysters were *afraid*? But somewhere we know exactly what he means, and we see how aptly he has employed the word, and we see those delicate edges retracting when the lemon juice is squeezed on them. Hemingway, as we know, liked simple words, basic, strong words. Because of that, when he uses a more complicated word instead, it gets your attention. For example, he often uses "commence" instead of "begin" or "start." He says that when he first started writing, he "commenced with the basic things—birth, death, love." Mark Twain has Huck Finn use that word, too.

Here's an example by that lovely writer Isak Dinesen, from *Out of Africa,* a book even Holden Caulfield liked. She writes about shooting an iguana:

> In the Reserve I have sometimes come upon the Iguana, the big lizards, as they were sunning themselves upon a flat stone in a river-bed. They are not pretty in shape, but nothing can be imagined more beautiful than their colouring. They shine like a heap of precious stones or like a pane cut out of an old church window. When, as you ap-

proach, they swish away, there is a flash of azure, green and purple over the stones, the colour seems to be standing behind them in the air, like a comet's luminous tail.

Once I shot an Iguana. I thought that I should be able to make some pretty things from its skin. A strange thing happened then, that I have never afterwards forgotten. As I went up to him, where he was lying dead upon his stone, and actually while I was walking the few steps, he faded and grew pale, all colour died out of him as in one long sigh, and by the time that I touched him he was grey and dull like a lump of concrete. It was the live impetuous blood pulsating within the animal, which had radiated out all that glow and splendour. Now that the flame was put out, and the soul had flown, the Iguana was dead as a sandbag.

Well, the word I want to point out is "impetuous," but "sigh" is a beauty, too. The color "dying out of him in one long sigh." The word itself is like a soft exhale, and we can feel the life emptying from the animal then and there. The use of "azure" here is effective, too, in "a flash of azure." Exotic, like the animal. And flash-like in its saying.

Then there's the "live impetuous" blood. What does she mean by that? Well, the first definition of "impetuous" is, "marked by force and violence of movement or action." The word comes from the Latin *impetus,* meaning "attack, assault." So, she's emphasizing the force of the blood thrusting through the system. I think we have a tacit understanding of what she's saying, even if we aren't familiar with the primary meaning of the word, simply because of the word's *music,* the four, nearly equal syllables, beating out time like a pump. Also, the word, because it's a bit unusual, and therefore prominent, makes us concentrate on the animal's aliveness.

I don't know if you would agree that this is the exact word, but I can tell you I've never forgotten it.

I saw a production of Oscar Wilde's *Salomé* on Broadway in New York some time ago with Al Pacino, Marisa Tomei, and Dianne Wiest. It was fascinating. Pacino played Herod. Marisa Tomei was mesmerizing as Salomé. I was struck by what she kept saying to the stern, rebuking John the Baptist, "I will kiss your mouth, Jokanaan." She—or Wilde—doesn't say, "I will kiss your lips, Jokanaan" or, "I will kiss you, Jokanaan." She says, "I will kiss your *mouth*." Boy, does that go straight to the groin. Especially when Marisa Tomei says it. Thomas Hardy understood the power of the word "mouth," too. He uses it in *The Return of the Native* when he describes Eustacia Vye: "On Egdon, coldest and meanest kisses were at famine prices; and where was a mouth matching hers to be found?" Your inclination might be to think "lips" is sexier, especially when "mouth" is often associated with "loud" and dental hygiene. But "lips" isn't sexier; "mouth" is. And you know it when you see it, or read it. This is one of the great pleasures of reading: that communication between you and the writer—almost a complicity—where you both understand precisely what's going on here. In this case, it's how sexual these mouths are, how mortally sexual.

So, I would say, trust the word, and not necessarily what it's become accepted to mean or to imply.

The complicated word, or complex word, can the right one, too. Here's one I like from Gilbert White's lovely book, *The Natural History of Selborne*. White was a parson who lived in England in the mid-eighteenth century, and his book, really a series of letters, was first published in 1789. He describes a mouse's nest as "this wonderful procreant cradle." *Procreant*. I may be putting a bit too much into this, but it seems to me the word has a bit of a gentle sag in the middle, like a hammock, where someone might nestle. (Update: In doing research for another essay, I found that White had taken the expression "procreant cradle" from *Macbeth*. Well, he knew a good phrase when he saw one.)

No writer came at words from such oblique angles, and put them to better use, than Marianne Moore. If you haven't read her prose, especially her essay on writing, "Humility, Concentration and Gusto," I urge you to. She knew more than a thing or two about good writing, and I can't for the life of me understand why she isn't referred to more in the new legion of books about writing that gets bigger by the moment. She says of style, for example, "Originality is any case a by-product of sincerity." But the example I want is when she says, "If emotion is strong enough, the words are unambiguous." What a deft way of using that word, *unambiguous*. I think what makes this so emphatic is that what she wants to say about the words is contained in one word, instead of two. Instead of saying, for example, "the words are not ambiguous," she economizes and, in a single word, gives us an example of precisely what she means. "Not ambiguous" somehow implies the possibility of ambiguity. What an insight to see that difference! Now, I don't think you arrive at this kind of choice quickly, or easily. Our instincts, I believe, would be *not* to choose "unambiguous." That's why I think reading is so important. It will show you things you didn't think could be done (or you didn't think you could do) and that can be done.

Moore, by the way, was one of the least snobbish writers when she wrote about writing. She quotes from any and every source—even from a Treasury Department memo.

One final so-called complex word. This is from John Cheever's splendid, moving book, *Falconer*. He speaks of "the utter poverty of erotic reasonableness." That word "reasonableness" affixed to "erotic" for me summons up all the cold, patterned sex one has experienced and the lack of hope found there. Cheever knew a lot about that. It's hard to read his journals and read about his having to barter with his wife for sex—he offering to buy something for her if, as he wrote, "she would let me have my way with her." Reason and Eros side by side. Where can you find a more unhappy couple?

Sometimes writers use words to describe something that couldn't happen, but nevertheless they *make* it happen. Truman Capote is describing a ride on horseback in his book *Breakfast at Tiffany's*,

> Very gently the horses began to trot, waves of wind splashed us, spanked our faces, we plunged in and out of sun and shadow pools, and joy, a glad-to-be-alive exhilaration jolted through me like a jigger of nitrogen.

Now, very few of us have downed a jigger of nitrogen, but that doesn't matter, does it? We know what Capote means. I love the word "jigger," too. It's a word that immediately evokes one quick lethal shot of firewater thrown back and shooting through the system. The word takes you directly to your hand picking up a shot glass.

You probably don't get to "jigger" on the first try. Maybe you *need* a jigger to get to it. But it's out there, waiting, and Capote has reassured you it is.

I'd like to talk a little about prepositions.

How can a little preposition be a candidate for the exact word? I think the answer is the Gettysburg Address. Lincoln was, truly, a marvelous writer, and all you have to do is read his letters to prove it. In any case, at the end of his speech Lincoln says the words we all know,

> It is rather for us to be here dedicated to the great task remaining before us—that from these honored dead we take increased devotion to that cause for which they gave the last full measure of devotion—that we here highly resolve that these dead shall not have died in vain—that this nation, under God, shall have a new birth of freedom—and that government of the people, by the people, for the people, shall not perish from the earth.

Of the people, *by* the people, *for* the people.

Of, by, for. The preposition that really hits home for me is "of." That government *of* the people. Not from. *Of*. That our democracy flows out *of* who we are. As if it's…inalienable.

I think it's not only the first meaning of words we should be aware of, but what's inside them. We should be aware of their anatomy, what makes them stand up and have life. And they do have life! What did Emerson write about the American vernacular—"Cut these words & they would bleed." The etymology rests inside the word like a kernel inside a seed, and it has the same genealogical potency as a seed's kernel. A seed has within it the whole history of its species. So does a word. This is its secret power. As Milan Kundera writes in *The Unbearable Lightness of Being,* "The secret strength of its [a word's] etymology floods the word with another light and gives it a broader meaning." (Metaphors are mixing here, so fasten your seatbelts.) I think that can be a reason, maybe a subtle reason, for choosing one word over another—or at least a contributing factor. Let's say you were down to a choice between "mystery" and "enigma." As in the sentence, "Her carefree behavior following her beloved husband's death was a mystery." Or: "Her carefree behavior following her beloved husband's death was an enigma."

Which one?

Of course you have to consider the definitions. "Mystery," the dictionary says, is "something that has not been or cannot be explained." "Enigma" is an "inexplicable, circumstance, event or occurrence." But let's go to the secret meaning. "Mystery" goes back to the Greek *mystos,* which means, "to initiate into religious rites," which in turn comes from the Greek word *myein,* "to close the lips or eyes." "Enigma" is also from a Greek word, *ainigma,* which means, "to speak in riddles," which in turn is derived from the Greek *ainos,* "tale or fable."

So, what about it? Do we go with "close the lips or eyes?" Or with "speaking in riddles?" Will it be: "Her carefree behavior following her beloved husband's death was a mystery." Or: "Her carefree behavior following her beloved husband's death was an enigma." I really do believe this counts in trying to find the exact word, and sometimes can even be the deciding factor. It doesn't always play a significant role, but I think it's important to know what rests inside the word, because that's a lot of history, energy and creativity lurking. A lot of concentrated power. Why not use it?

We'll explore this more fully in the next chapter.

Finding the exact word is often a hunt, like looking for the Holy Grail, as Birkerts says, which, in legend, always seems to be over the next ridge. Sometimes, you have to follow your leads down all the tributaries and dead ends until you get what you want. I like to look up the definition of a word, even if I think I know it, because usually I don't know it as well as I think I do. Then I like to look at the synonyms, because though I'm sure in general what I want to say, I'm not sure exactly *how* I want to say it. Here are the shades of meanings, one word emphasizing one aspect of the idea, another word another. I usually look up the synonyms, too, because I probably don't know them as well as I think I do, and, besides, there might be something, some word, in the definition that might be what I'm looking for. It's impossible for me to carry all this inside my head, so I have to go through this process. Even Stephen Sondheim uses a rhyming dictionary.

As a reader, it's pure pleasure seeing a writer come up with word you just *know* is right. Like Mark Twain at the beginning of *Huckleberry Finn*. Poor Huck is grousing about living with the stern Widow Douglas. He says,

> The Widow Douglas, she took me for her son, and allowed she would sivilize me; but it was rough living in the house all the time, considering how dismal regular and decent the widow was in all her ways.

"Dismal regular and decent."

The word this laugh turns on is "dismal" modifying "decent." I laugh every time.

In the end, is it worth it? Well, we know the answer. But I want to go back to the master, Gustave Flaubert. Here's what he wrote someone about working on *Madame Bovary*, the book that gave him so much pain:

> Last Wednesday I had to get up and fetch my handkerchief; tears were streaming down my face. I had been moved by my own writing: the emotion I had conceived, the phrase that rendered it, and the satisfaction of having found the phrase—all were causing me the most exquisite pleasure.

3

The Secret Strength of Words

"The secret strength of its [a word's] etymology floods the word with another light and gives it a broader meaning"—Milan Kundera, The Unbearable Lightness of Being

A word is a seed. It's alive, like the seed of a plant or tree. Inside, is its entire history. If you could cut it open like the seed of a plant, you'd see wonderful things. Or, better yet, if you could examine its DNA or its genetics, you'd find thousands of changes and contributions distinguishing the rocky, creative path from its beginnings to its present recognizable form. Different forces of nature created a word than those that created the oak's acorn, but there is a kind of Darwinism at work here, as well. Words evolve. And still do evolve. Occasionally, they spring forth from a creator's mouth fully formed, and we call them coined words ("serendipity" is one, from Horace Walpole's *The Three Princes of Serendip*), but, for the most part, a word takes a languid, fish-to-lizard journey that, while not requiring millions of years, may indeed require hundreds before it's fully realized and in the form we recognize.

Why bother? Why bother thinking or musing about what's inside, or behind, a word? Just *use* it. Well, yes, but as the title of the chapter implies, and as Milan Kundera says, there is a secret strength in a word's etymology. Knowledge, as we know, is power, and so our knowledge of what's inside a word increases our power as writers. We understand the word better, like a person, if we know its background and its roots. When we know why and how it was created—in so far as we can—we have an added resource when we write where "every attempt / Is a wholly new start," as T. S. Eliot said.

Fortunately, we don't have to be a literary botanist or geneticist, or any kind of expert, to explore a word's roots. We have very capable people who have done that for us, and the results of this digging are there for us to see in a good dictionary. If we want to explore in more detail, there are books specifically dedicated to etymology that will let us do that. Every definition of a word in a respectable dictionary has a brief description of the word's etymology.

And why don't we start with the word itself, with *etymology*. It gets to the heart of the matter, or at least to one of its chambers. Here's what my favorite dictionary, an old and trusted friend, the *Random House Unabridged*, Second Edition, says. First, the definition of the word *etymology:*

1.   the derivation of a word. 2. an account of the history of a particular word or element of a word.

Now, the etymology of *etymology*:

[1350-1400; ME < L *etymologia* < Gk *etymología,* eqiv. To *etymoló(os)* studying the true meanings and values of words (*étymo(s)* true + *logos* word, reason)

Notice: "meanings and values." The Greek *etymon* means "the essential meaning of a word." So that we might say that *etymology*, from its very beginnings, has been closely associated with the idea of *truth.* At its very core, is the idea of "meanings and values," a search for "the essential meaning." Therefore, when I look into the derivation, the etymology, of a word, I am a truth-seeker. The simple meaning isn't enough. I should seek the values that formed that word; I should seek its essential meaning. It's a kind of ethical or moral pursuit. The creation—not to say the use—of words is inextricably linked to human values. This it seems to me is one great difference between the study of the origins of species and the origins of words: it's an ethical one.

An etymologist, professional or dedicated amateur, then, is an ethicist.

By bothering to split open a word, I believe I have a profounder understanding of the abstract concept or specific object that the word represents. And, more important, of the human struggle, perhaps environmental, perhaps ideological, that prompted its creation.

Since our language is like a tree with a vast, wide system of roots that are spread across tracts of water and land, the derivations of words have characteristics of a variety of landscapes and humanity. Words with Greek derivations often have roots in *philosophy*—that word, for example—in the idea of man's place in the world, as one might expect. Words like *democracy, theology, theory.* Words with Latin roots often have a ring of the official or the administrative, as befits a vast, strictly efficient empire. Words like *rational, legislation, consequence.* Words with Anglo-Saxon births are often bluntly poetic, wonderfully hard and harsh, with lasting power and presence, as if they'd been hewn out of glacial rock with an ax. They are often words connected to violence, aggression, power, force, physicality, and to the harsh weather and land where these people lived. They often refer to the basic actions of the body, of the arms, legs, lips, eye, and heart. They are words like *blow, run, dig, hurt, strike, kill, eat, stink.* They are us at our most basic.

Greek-derived words are often amalgams of other Greek words that already existed—like the two words that make up *etymology.* But where did *they* come from? How does one come up with *étymos* for "truth"? Or, specifically, the meaning, "true, actual, real." How does one signify a *sound* for such an abstract concept? How does one even understand what the idea of *truth* or *true* is? Then, how does one verbalize that? These were artists who created these types of words. Philosophers and artists. So, here we have the Greeks struggling with the idea of truth, and with ideas and existential questions in a way hardly equaled since, and certainly never more emphatically, except for perhaps in the eighteenth century.

The Latin words we have incorporated into our language speak to the need in us to have an order; they speak to the mind, too, and not so much the heart. When, and why, would we use the word *pulchritude*?

The Anglo-Saxon words speak to the cold necessity of survival.

After using words for some time, and listening to them, absorbing them, we are able to say, with some exactitude, what part of the world a word derived from. We can often sense its pedigree.

Words are collaborations. Very few words in history have been created by one person. They are efforts of multiple personalities. We know that because there is a derivation. There is a progression that can be traced. It's not an exact science, but there is a trail, nevertheless, that can be followed from one stage to another. So in that sense words are quite democratic. They not only belong to us, they were created by us. They are the result of many anonymous minds and voices, each honing the sound and meaning through the centuries until it finally seemed there was nothing left to hone any more. As the *Webster's New World Dictionary* so aptly says in its essay on etymology, "Seen as the product of perhaps three thousand years of human experience, a word may have not only many facets, but may somehow reflect with brilliant intensity the concentrated experience or insights of the generations." Even *malapropism,* which comes from a character in a play by Richard Brinsley

Sheridan, Mrs. Malaprop, a lady who has the tendency to misuse words, or near-misuse them, in memorable ways (she spoke of "allegories on the Nile")—even that word wasn't invented by Sheridan, but, rather, by a Mr. or Ms. Anonymous who used the character as a basis for coining the new word.

Wouldn't it have been fascinating to have been there when a new word was born, its desire to be born thrusting it through the shell that encased it, cracking the sides of its woody confinement, then splitting it apart and emerging, flimsy at first, but then, eventually, firmer and thriving?

One of your—and my—ancestors, or several of them, no doubt contributed to the creation of a word, or words. They might not have fully comprehended what they were doing at the time, or maybe they did—who knows? I had a fantasy about this. My ancestors are Germanic, so I like to think that perhaps great great (etc.) grandfather, Ugar the Brutal, might have spent long hours struggling with a way to refer to, to name, what later became known as a *hut*. (I don't know why I picked that word. Just came to me.) I see from the dictionary that the word ultimately has its roots in the West Germanic word *hudjā,* whose meaning is akin to the verb, *to hide*.

I can identify with Ugar, as a matter of fact. I often use my twenty-first-century *hut*, i.e., my Manhattan apartment, to hide from the world. It's a pretty small *hut*, too. So there he is, my ancestor, trying to survive in a coarse, difficult world, with dangers all around him and his family. Perhaps the only place he can go is to that skin-covered dwelling he has built on a hill. There is no *word* for this place, however. There is only the word, *hudjā,* and every time he *hudjās,* every time he hides, it is in this skin-draped place. One day, he begins to use the word *hudjā* not only to mean the *action* of hiding, but the *place* where the action of hiding takes him. His family starts to use the word in the same way. Soon enough, his brothers and sisters and parents begin to understand that *hudjā* not only means to *hide*, but it also means that place where Ugar and his family go when it storms, when it's night, when it's cold, when it's threatening.

Ugar's relatives realize they don't have a word for their dwelling, either, and that maybe they can use this same word, too, for where they go to *hudjā*. So they do. *Hudjā,* meaning *hut*, is born. A few years later, many more people are using the new word, or, rather, using an old word with its new meaning. By then, everyone has forgotten that it was Ugar who started this trend. No matter how much he points to himself and jumps up and down when people use the word to mean *hut,* no one remembers, or really cares. Maybe someone else tries to take credit for *hudjā,* meaning *hut,* and perhaps they even are recognized as the creator and receive some sort of ceremonial recognition, the equivalent of a round of applause. Ugar, alas, dies a bitter, disillusioned artist, mumbling to himself, "I invented *hudjā*! *I* was the first one to use it that way—not Thorak!"

Note: We remember the word *hide* is not only a verb, but a noun. *Hides* are skins of animals, and it turns out that the derivation of this word is Old High German *hut* and that it is akin to the verb, "to hide." In other words, skins, *hides,* provided shelter but also a *place* "to hide," and so that place became a *hut.* The word might have developed in that fashion.

I think, as Thomas Pynchon reminded us recently, it's good to be grateful for "this English idiom we are blessed to have inherited." It's good to think of all those anonymous builders and shapers of words who did their part through the ages to bring this great language into full being.

I was thinking of Borges's fascination with, and love of, Anglo-Saxon, and how delighted he was with discovering that, in *Beowulf,* the Anglo-Saxon word for *sea* is "whale road," *hronrade.* As a poet, as a writer, of course this would excite him. What a metaphor! It turns things on their heels. The sea does not belong to we humans, but is—and here we name it—a *highway* for enormous swimming mammals. The implication is that here we have peoples who, despite their lack of mercy, were capable of outright awe, of perspective, of knowing their place in the world. Though often murderous, they understood the sea was a place where boats were, at best, uninvited guests.

Human frailty, human politics, human weakness and human short sightedness are there for one to see in some of our words' histories as well. Since the creation and development of a word is a human endeavor, it must be marked with human shortcomings as well. A Greek-derived word provides an example—*hysterical.* It comes from the word *hysterikós,* which means, "suffering in the womb." The *Random House Unabridged Dictionary* elaborates: "reflecting the Greeks' belief that hysteria was peculiar to women and caused by disturbances in the uterus." If you have a womb, you are not in control of your emotions. Men, presumably, are not subject to *hysteria.* Women are hysterical because they have a womb. So even back then, from these most intelligent of peoples, we have a gender-biased word. Like *lunacy,* the state of being made mad because of the moon's influence, it derives more from fear and prejudice than from facts.

By thinking of those people who created bits of sound that could be repeated to others reliably, we link ourselves to the tidal struggle of what it means to be human. We link ourselves to the effort of trying to make sense and order of an often perplexing world in which we live. To imagine this is to feel a responsibility. I think that, as with the seeds of plants and trees, we are the stewards of words.

I'm more often wrong about the definition of a word than I'd like to be. And if I knew more about the word's derivation, I might not make that many mistakes. Take the word *holocaust.* With a capital H, we all know it refers to the deliberate mass killings of Jews by the Nazis in World War II. But somehow I had in mind that the word meant a kind of natural disaster, like a hurricane, I suppose. I always found it odd that such a calculated event had affixed to it a word that signified blameless nature. I was wrong. The word means, "a great or complete devastation or destruction, esp. by fire." The second definition is, "a sacrifice completely consumed by fire; burnt offering." A shudder went through me when I read that. The etymology? From the Greek *holókaustos,* meaning "burnt whole." Someone knew what they were doing when they chose that word.

Etymology can not only throw new light upon a word, it can change the way you use that word. Take the word *kill. Kill* is with us every day, and has been since the earth was born. In the early part of Genesis, we have a murder: Cain kills Abel. Well, the dictionary tells us that *kill* has strong associations with the word *quell.* You can hear that. The *RHUD* tells us that *quell* came into written English before 900 AD, even before *kill.* The word is defined as "to suppress, to put an end to, extinguish." Its origins go back to Old Norse, *kvelja,* to torment, and also to the Old English *cwellan,* to kill.

Now I see the word "quell" differently. It's more *deadly* than it was to me before. Up until now it seemed a word that was a bit on the light side, compared to say, *stop.* Now, I look forward to finding just the right time and place for it, when I can use its added strength, its implication of *kill.* I can actually feel the idea of *kill* in *quell.* I don't see it as a lightweight word any more. I'm going to quell that opinion I had right now. This knowledge of the word's soul helps me in my writing. It helps me in my choices, and in my desire to use words correctly and creatively. Does a reader understand this? Does a reader feel *any* of this? I believe he or she does. I believe a great deal of communication in writing, of our understanding of prose, is implicit, as well as explicit. Which, I believe, is how we understand all art.

Some etymologies are mysteries, and that can be vexing (Note to self: look up the derivation of *vexing*). I just randomly came upon the word "odonate," meaning belonging or pertaining to the order Odonata, which comprises the damselflies and dragonflies. The derivation? Neo Latin (i.e., some modern-day Linnaeus), Odonata, from the Greek, *odón*, "tooth." What? Do dragonflies have teeth? Does any insect have teeth? Mandibles, maybe, but teeth? And even if they did, wouldn't another characteristic—say those webby, filmy wings—be more suitable for a Latin name? Wouldn't Odonata be a better name for, say, *tigers* or *sharks?* Now, those animals have teeth. I called the American Museum of Natural History, and a scientist in the Entomology Department said that, well, he wasn't exactly sure. He thought that it might refer to a portion of an insect's abdomen that looks like a tooth. He suspected, however, that it was because of the insects' large mandibles.

Hold on. In the *Entomology* Department? I had to check to see if this word is any relation to *etymology.* In fact, there is a world of difference between *entomo(s)-* and *etymos-*. Remember that *etymos* means "true." Well, *éntomos* means "notched," presumably referring to the abdomens of insects or their segmented bodies—e.g., those "notched" caterpillars, for example. Well, I had to check.

I asked another expert, Dr. Thomas Sappington, an insect ecologist in Iowa State University's Entomology Department, about this vexing word, *Odonata.* Here's his take:

> I'm not entirely sure about the derivation of the word, but dragonflies do not have teeth. My best guess is that the derivation is from "Odo" meaning "a way" or "swollen" in Greek, and "nat" meaning rump in Latin. Some insects in this order indeed have a "swollen rump" as adults, in that the ovipositor (egg laying apparatus) is on the underside of the abdomen near the tip, giving it a swollen appearance in females. However, that is just a semi-educated guess. "Nata" means "birth" in Latin, but I don't know how that would match up with the meanings of "Odo," You are correct that "Odon" means "tooth," but as far as I know, "ata" doesn't mean anything, so "Odo" probably is the correct root.

I have a feeling this could go on and on. It's a kind of madness, once you get going. The point is, I think, that some etymologies get lost along the way. Experts will make their best educated guesses, and in some cases, coming to a derivational dead end, place a question mark at the close of their etymological entry. They just don't know. When you think about it, it's really a kind of miracle that they *do* know anything about where a word derives from. It's not as if you had people taking notes while the slow, indefinite process of development was taking place.

You will often see writers, particularly essayists, make a point about a concept by introducing the etymology of a word, its root. In the November 30, 2006 issue of the *New York Review of Books,* for example, an essay by Michael Tomasky about Barack Obama titled, "The Phenomenon," begins:

> The word "phenomenon"—from the Greek word *phainesthai,* "to appear," and related to another Greek word that is the root of the English word "fantasy"—possesses a unique potency in our culture. While scientists may use it to mean anything observable, it is popularly applied to rock stars, movie stars, top athletes, and the like. Even today, in our hype-drenched society, it is not used promiscuously. It is reserved for that special minority of people who seem to have singular talent and potential; for those with the ability, that is, to fulfill our collective fantasies.

Here we see that the author wants us, his readers, to know that he has chosen the title of his essay very carefully, and that he means to use the root of the word "phenomenon," its essence, as a springboard for talking about Barack Obama's qualities.

Sven Birkerts, in his book *The Gutenberg Elegies: The Fate of Reading in an Electronic Age,* begins an essay, "The Shadow Life of Reading," this way: "Reading: the term is as generous and imprecise as 'love.' So often it means more than just the word-by-word deciphering of the printed page. Although that definition is primary, the word's etymology (from the Anglo-Saxon *raedan,* 'to make out, to interpret') points us toward the open sea. We use the verb freely to denote diverse and nonspecific involvements with texts." Here, too the fulcrum of his point rests squarely on the essential meaning of the word.

When writing about Montaigne, essayists inevitably point to the fact that the word for "essay" derives from the French word, *essai,* which means "attempts" or "trials," thus implying imperfection, reaching, a quest for understanding. I take this knowledge to guide me in my essays which I hopefully see as mere attempts, mere *essays*, to understand something a little bit better.

I noticed in the delightful book, *One Hundred Birds and How They Got Their Names* by Diana Wells, that a mystery about a bird's name was solved by the etymology of the name. She was examining the Ruby-Throated Hummingbird and its scientific name, *Archilochus colubris*. It turns out that the word *Archilochus* derives from an actual person, a seventh-century BC Greek poet. This stumped Wells. She researched

Archilochus' life and found that, aside from his fame as a poet, he had been branded as a coward for running away during battle. One night, the author sat up in bed—presumably shouting out *Eureka!*—realizing that the hummingbird is the only bird that can fly *backwards.* So it was named after a man who *ran* backwards. The irony is that the hummingbird is far from being a coward, and is, in fact, quite intrepid, its little frame flying great distances over open seas during its migratory period as well as fiercely defending its territory from unwanted rivals. Anyone who has ever witnessed hummingbirds battle in the air will have seen quite a vicious struggle indeed. There is no backing down among them.

I remember one writer who, in an essay about traveling, reminded his readers that the word *travel* has the same root as the word *travail*, which ultimately means "torture." That is: *travel* implies hard times, difficulty. The point he was trying to make was that genuine travelers should experience some difficulty in getting to where they want to go, or they really aren't *traveling.* This, then, goes back to the point I was trying to establish at the beginning of the chapter. That is, if you are looking for the etymology of a word, you are looking for "meanings and values" and for "the essential meaning" of a word. You want to get at the truth of the matter, to the heart of the matter.

Thoreau begins his essay "Walking" with a paean to the etymology of the word *sauntering.* He writes:

> I have met with but one or two persons in the course of my life who understood the art of Walking, that is, of taking walks,—who had a genius, so to speak for *sauntering*: which word is beautifully derived "from idle people who roved about the country, in the Middle Ages, and asked charity, under the pretense of going *à la Sainte Terre*," to the Holy Land, till the children exclaimed, "There goes a *Sainte-Terrer*," a Saunterer, a Holy-Lander.

Then he cites another possibility for the word's source:

> Some, however, would derive the word from *sans terre*, without land or home, which, therefore, in the good sense, will mean, having no particular home, but equally at home everywhere. For this is the secret of successful sauntering. He who sits still in a house all the time may be the greatest vagrant of all; but the saunterer, in the good sense, is no more vagrant than the meandering river, which is all the while sedulously seeking the shortest course to the sea. But I prefer the first, which, indeed, is the most probable derivation. For every walk is a sort of crusade....

I take that one phrase, "having no particular home, but equally at home everywhere," to be one of Thoreau's most concise self-portraits. The essay continues, building upon the basic idea culled from the word's derivation: that walking is a sort of holy enterprise, "to reconquer this

Holy Land from the Infidels." This is an entire essay built upon the true meaning of a word, upon its essence. Thoreau wants us to see that every walk is a kind of pilgrimage. He concludes the essay by returning to this idea, "So we saunter toward the Holy Land, till one day the sun shall shine more brightly than ever he has done…and light up our whole lives with a great awakening light."

The first chapter of Henry Miller's book, *The Books in My Life,* is titled, "They Were Alive And They Spoke To Me." This is how I believe we should see words. Some of what they have to say to us are powerful secrets, and they can only be heard by looking inside them, by awakening them, and by asking them to speak.

4

Some Things English Can't Do— and Shouldn't

English can't do everything. It can do a lot of wonderful things, but there are some things it just cannot do. It cannot make certain sounds, it can't express certain things, and it's ultimately limited in its musical range, as any language is. The fact is that it *shouldn't* do everything.

A language is tied to the people who speak it, and vice-versa. So it's more than just a repository of words that are used as tools in communication. It's the story of a culture. A language is a country's heritage, its patrimony. It's the accumulated grace and creativity of a people. It represents efforts to express and to mark and to signify over many hundreds of years, but within the context of a people's way of living. The words and expressions the French, Syrians, and Malaysians have developed are different not only because they have different linguistic roots but because their peoples have lived different lives.

There is linguistic and cultural history in the difference between the Spanish word for butter, *mantequilla,* and ours. Lives led differently produce different sounds. A people has a personality, an attitude, a philosophy, and this is manifested in their language. It's not just that English isn't Spanish because of the grammar and vocabulary and structure of the language. It's also that English speakers have not seen and experienced the world precisely the same way as Spanish speakers. *Mantequilla,* which means "butter" in Spanish, (pronounced mahn-tah-KEY-ah) derives from the Spanish word *manteca,* which means "fat." Its origins are pre-Roman—from a people indigenous to Spain before the Roman Empire. Our word for this fat-based substance we spread on bread ultimately derives from the ancient Greek, *boútūron.* These two words are different not by some semantic accident, but by culture. As the translator Gregory Rabassa wrote, "I contend that the sound of a language must come from the cultural expression and evolution of a people."

Each language has its linguistic triumphs, its syntactical marvels and beauties, its eccentricities and powers that are unique to that language. Some of them are profound.

Some of these are pure pleasure to see and to hear; some are astonishing.

Vladimir Nabokov said that the three most beautiful languages are Russian, French, and English. He knew all of them well, having been raised learning them. He knew some German, too, having lived in Berlin for a while, but he was not as confident with that language. He *was* clearly confident with the big trio. One might say arrogantly so, and he was forever correcting translators. All you have to do is dip into his *Lectures on Literature* and look at the reproductions of his copies of the books he was lecturing on and read his notations. Many of them are slaps on the hands of the translators with the correct English words written over theirs, sometimes with acerbic comments. He even writes of Madame Bovary's "dreadfully translated" hairdo: "This hairdo has been so dreadfully translated in all versions that the correct description must be given else one cannot visualize her correctly." This he proceeds to do.

Nabokov had enough Spanish to declare *mariposa,* "butterfly," a gorgeous word. He would know that word, being the world-class lepidopterist that he was. You cannot say *mariposa,* and have it mean something, except in Spanish. It's pronounced—and here I wish a great speaker of Spanish would appear by magic to say it the way it should be said—"mar-ee-PŌS-ah." *Mariposa!* I'm not certain everyone finds *mariposa* beautiful, though I'd ask anyone to *say* the word before he or she comes to a conclusion. The question of a word's (or anything's) "beauty" is as complex as the word beauty itself. Some words are more amusing than they are gorgeous; some are wittier than they are pretty. We receive the beauty of the immense sinuousness of the Great Wall of China differently than the playful mathematics of a Paul Klee painting. But the word beauty can certainly be applied to both. A word in Spanish like *aunque*, "although," delights because of what the mouth has to do in order to say it. It has to twist and contort like a thrown lasso to say, Ah-YOON-kay. Its beauty and pleasure are of a different sort than *mariposa*'s. I love to say *mantequilla*, because I think it's pretty, but also because it means "butter." Part of the pleasure of saying the Italian word, *francobollo* is, I think, that it means "postage stamp."

Beginning at the beginning, with the individual. You might write an entire essay—or at least have a spirited conversation—on the first person pronoun in English and in Spanish. In Spanish, it's *Yo*. In English, *I*. Yo is pronounced, well, *Yo,* to rhyme with *no*. I, of course, is pronounced *eye*. The mouth is shaped differently in speaking these two words, and the sounds produced are different. The *music* is different. It's as if one were playing with a flute on the one hand and a guitar on the other. *I* seems to emanate from the nose. *Yo* comes from the chest. Since the concept of "I" is so basic, when you have a linguistic and aural difference as basic as that between *I* and *Yo,* you can sense a philosophical difference in the languages as well.

Picasso painted two remarkable self-portraits in 1901. One is titled, *Yo, Picasso*. The other is, simply, *Yo*. The "Y" in *Yo* even *looks* like a person, standing, arms spread in a "Here I am!" stance. You can annunciate *Yo* with much more force than *I*. You can shout the word "I," but it hits a high register. But you can *thunder Yo*. You can say it with deep rolling power. You can say it defiantly, with a sense of reckoning.

During the latter part of his reign, Philip IV, patron of Velazquez, and witness to the decline of the Spanish empire, wrote letters to a nun in a convent, probably to get his mind off everything collapsing around him. He signed the letters, simply, *Yo, el Rey*. I, the King. *This is Spanish.* Drama, force, directness. Spanish looks you in the eye. When you speak Spanish, you feel like attacking bulls, or windmills.

What's slightly contradictory and somewhat puzzling is that often in Spanish native speakers will leave out the first person pronoun—in fact, leave out pronouns altogether. (You cannot do this in French.) It's common to hear, for example, a Spanish speaker say "I believe that" as *Creo que,* instead of *Yo creo que*. I'm not sure exactly what this means, if it means anything at all—though I think every linguistic "decision" has some meaning somewhere—but it seems paradoxical to have such a simple, strong, assertive first person pronoun, perhaps the strongest there is, and to drop it altogether, to put it away in a trunk somewhere. Are the Spanish disarming themselves in a way so as not to be so forcefully self-promoting? Are they de-*Yo*-ing themselves to say, look, *I* don't want to come on too strong? Are they shy about using the full force of *Yo?* Or is it much simpler? Is it the linguistic equivalent of the French eliminating the "ne" in their negatives? Instead of saying, correctly, *Je ne mange pas*, "I don't eat," most will simply say, *Je mange pas*, sloughing off the *ne* like the skin of an orange.

Continuing with the *Yo*-I discussion. In French, the first person pronoun is *Je*. The differences in this case are even greater than between

Spanish and English. You cannot, in French, use *Je* in the same way or in the same situations as the Spanish *Yo*. Each looks different, sounds different, and behaves differently. *Je* is pronounced *zhuh*. In the example of the Picasso painting, the difference is even more pronounced. You cannot say, *Je, Picasso*. It would have to be *Moi, Picasso*. A world of difference. (You could continue this comparison with the plurals of the first person pronoun, with the French *nous* and the Spanish *nosotros*.)

To me, an ideal way to spend an afternoon would be to talk to a native Spanish speaker about the fundamental differences between our two languages. What history did he or she think shaped the language? Is there something at the very core of Spanish or French he or she can identify that bespeaks a philosophy of a people? This is a subject where I wish I had far more learning. The shelves of libraries humble you with the delicious, arcane depth of the books about semantics, linguistics, and the origins of language.

As I have said, each language has its own genius, something it does better than any other language. French, for example, has a genius for expressing abstract modes of human behavior, for describing how people *act*. If you start with the simple expression, *touché,* you can get a good idea of the language's wit and skill. It refers to fencing, and is an acknowledgement that you have "touched" your opponent with your sword, or *épée*, thus gaining a point. As an expression, though, it is an acknowledgement that you have made a particularly sharp or effective comment. Someone says something so apt, that couldn't be said better, and so you acknowledge it with *touché!* The word carries with it the force of a deft thrust of a blade—there is both skill and potential harm involved in the words that were said and acknowledged. That the comment is physical in its nature, that it goes directly to the body, to the corpus of the person, is implied.

All of us have experienced a moment when someone says something to us in response to something we said, or did, that is so right, so undeniable, so inescapable, that we feel it go directly *into* our body. We blush, we cringe, we blink, we stammer, we're speechless. It's the French genius to see this, and to find a way of expressing it perfectly. We don't say *touché* much anymore—it seems out of a nineteenth-century novel and somewhat affected. But when we do—and sometimes we just can't help ourselves—we have a quick, small understanding of the genius of the French language. It's the perfect, the only thing to say. It's an acknowledgement and a kind of surrender. There is an understanding that you have been bettered by words. English can't do that nearly as well. As Gregory Rabassa noted, "Some concepts seem to be the exclusive property of one language and cannot be rightly conceived in another."

Not only that—and this is a common characteristic of the best of the French expressions—*touché* is brilliantly concise. In fact, concision is at the heart of all the most memorable French expressions. Concision, and an almost pictorial wit. Some of these expressions almost seem as if they were constructed by Le Nôtre, the creator of Louis XIV's geometrically perfect gardens at Versailles. They *look* witty. You can see that with an expression like *arrière-pensée,* which means "hidden motive." Literally translated, it means "behind-thought." So there you have it: the expression is sculpted to convey there is something, literally, *behind,* the thought that is being presented for its face value. Behind that, is another thought, the *real* thought. Look at the expression: the word *arrière* is actually holding up, bolstering, the word *pensée,* so that, visually, it is clear that this is the stronger, the more prominent concept. The closest we have to this is "ulterior motive." At their best, the qualities of French expressions are just as much visual as they are verbal. You look at the words and you see the meaning, the inference, at the same time as you ingest the meaning of the word or words.

Because French often places its modifiers after its nouns, there is a kind of poetry that English cannot, because of how it works, achieve. So, for example, there is the French expression, *l'heure bleue,* which refers to that often shimmering time between the hours of daylight and darkness. We say "the magic hour" for that concept. It's sort of sad to write that next to *l'heure bleue.* French knows what to do here. French knows that the concept of "blue" is critical; that time of soft, subtle waning is about hue. French knows that emphasis should be on the idea of blue, but also that sufficient strength is given to the idea of the hour, to *l'heure. L'heure bleue* sounds like subtle magic.

Every so often the right book comes along as precisely the right time, almost as if it were fulfilling a need you couldn't express. *The Meaning of Tingo and Other Extraordinary Words From Around the World* by Adam Jacot de Boinod is such a book. It's a little tome, barely over two hundred pages, and small in size at that, but it contains many delights. It's a compilation of unusual, amusing, and surprising words that literally span the globe, and while there is great fun in reading the book, it's also mighty instructive as well. "My interest in the quirkiness of foreign words was triggered," writes de Boinod, "when one day, working as a researcher for the BBC quiz programme *QI,* I picked up a weighty Albanian dictionary to discover that they have no fewer than twenty-seven words for eyebrows and the same number for moustache."

De Boinod goes on to present some "wonderful words" from "the Fuegian of the southernmost Chile to the Inuit of northernmost Alaska, and from the Maori of the remote Cook Islands to Siberian Yakut." What the author found were words that could *only* have come out of a particular culture, such as *nakhur,* "a Persian word (which may not even be known to most native speakers) meaning 'a camel that won't give milk until her nostrils have been tickled.'" But he also found words like *touché*—though much more amusing—that express sentiments we have but that English does not capture in a single word. As he writes, "Haven't we all felt *termangu-mangu,* Indonesian for 'sad and not sure what to do' or *mukamuka,* Japanese for 'so angry one feels like throwing up'?" *The Meaning of Tingo* is a highly entertaining argument for understanding a country's culture through its language. And for maintaining linguistic differences.

Writers often become enamored of foreign languages and try to imitate, or mimic, the cadence and the flavor of a foreign language when they write in English. Hemingway did this all the time, most particularly in *For Whom the Bells Tolls* and *The Old Man and the Sea.* In the former, he tries to transpose the familiar form of "you"—*tu*—to English, using "thee" and "thou." It sounds somewhat stilted, as if the characters were Quakers, but he was trying to convey something about the Spanish *language* to his readers. He was trying to see if he could take that use of the familiar—which exists in other romance languages as well—and import its significance and subtlety into his novel. It *means* something when you speak to another person in the familiar form, particularly in French. It's extremely intimate, and touching. Hemingway wanted to capture that, because, one would assume, he appreciated it.

In *The Old Man and the Sea,* he uses the way one describes things in Spanish to comic effect, in what is now a famous part of the book where the characters are talking about baseball:

> "The Yankees cannot lose."
> "But I fear the Indians of Cleveland."
> "Have faith in the Yankees, my son. Think of the great DiMaggio."
> "I fear both the Tigers of Detroit and the Indians of Cleveland."
> "Be careful or you will fear even the Reds of Cincinnati and the White Sox of Chicago."

This is affectionate, and warm, and funny. Hemingway was, of course, in giving a literal translation of the talk, trying to bestow on the prose a unique sense of authenticity, as he was in *For Whom the Bell Tolls*. But he is also cleverly pointing out what Spanish does and what English does not do. Ultimately, this passage is as much about language as it is about baseball. Hemingway loved the Spanish language, spoke it brilliantly according to those who heard him, and understood it as perhaps few American writers ever have. This knowledge of Spanish, and his knowledge of French and Italian—both of which he knew at least passably well—made him a fuller writer, a richer writer, I think, and helped make him Hemingway.

Henry James, fluent in French, and obviously mad about the tongue, sprinkled his prose with French, like seeds. His assumption was that any civilized reader would know what those phrases meant, and that was true of his circle, but it's no longer true. He was more of a European writer than an American writer, and you do not find those French seeds in the writing of his contemporary, Mark Twain. So it's somewhat irritating to come upon these French words and expressions in Henry James, which are often not simple or well known, much like speed bumps on a lovely country road.

We are watching a glacier right now. The glacier is English, and it is moving with a steady inexorable force across the linguistic terrain of the world overwhelming everything in its path. More and more people are speaking English. The *New York Times* reported a few years back that some in Europe fear their languages are in peril. This is because English is the language of commerce. (Balzac said, "Money never misses the slightest occasion to demonstrate its stupidity.") If you want to do business on any scale, you need to speak English. English has become like one of those foreign species, an algae or ivy, that is introduced either by accident or with the foolish logic that it can eliminate some native pest. (Florida and France can attest to that misguided concept.) It destroys the native pest all right, but soon it takes over the entire lake or forest, strangling weaker competition and spreading its presence everywhere, until finally there is no more of the native species to be found.

Can we picture a France without French? Can we picture a future Nicolas Sarkozy speaking to the French public in English? That seems impossible, but as late as 1900 there were nearly ten million speakers of Provençal, which is a separate language entirely than French, part of the Occitan family, in the South of France. Many people spoke it exclusively, and did not, in fact, even know French. Twenty years later, there remained only a relative handful of Provençal speakers. The power of the French language, in this case imposed upon schools and curriculums, while at the same time Paris outlawed the use of Provençal in schools, did the trick. This shows the fragility of a language. Ten million speakers gone in a generation! The Basque language in Spain has about 1,000,000 speakers, and the number is declining. But the Basque people have steadfastly resisted much stronger restrictions against their language than the Provençal speakers ever had. They know that to lose their language would be catastrophic. For them, it's as much political as it is cultural. The language wars in Spain are fierce and meaningful. The Basque and Catalan people know the stakes are mortal.

In fact, in 1904, France's second Nobel Prize for literature went to the poet Frédéric Mistral (1830-1914) who wrote exclusively in Provençal. There is a story that as a young man he brought some of his first poems, which were written in French, to his mother who, not being able to read them—she read only Provençal—burst into tears. Mistral wrote only in Provençal after that. Mistral, along with six other writers, created the *Félibrige* society in 1854 to try to promote the Provençal language. Their efforts were mostly in vain, but as part of this campaign, Mistral, Samuel Johnson-like, compiled an enormous Provençal-French dictionary. Only a few scholars consult it today. Otherwise, it's a dead book for a dead language. Yet, two hundred years before Mistral, the young Parisian playwright Jean Racine (1639-1699), author of *Phèdre,* and one of the icons of French literature, visited the town of Uzès in the south of France, near Avignon, where his uncle lived. In one of his letters home he reports attending a trial and not understanding a word that was spoken. It was all in Provençal.

Today, no one speaks Provençal, except a handful of people, and many people have never even heard of it. The language is virtually gone, extinct, and with it the speakers' culture. Can English do that? Is it so immense as to be able to vanquish French or Italian? The news is bleak. Recently, the *New York Times* reported "of the estimated 7,000 languages spoken in the world today, linguists say nearly half are in danger of extinction and are likely to disappear in this century. In fact, they are falling out of use at a rate of about one every two weeks…at a rate, researchers said, that exceeds that of birds, mammals, fish or plants." English, with its global influence, is doing more than its part to insure that other, less influential languages disappear. You could argue that there is no conscious and official suppression of native languages by English, but I would maintain that the brute stupidity of money has the same effect in the end.

Before the Towel of Babel, "the whole earth was of one language, and of one speech," as it says in Genesis 11. Presumably, this was a desirable thing from the Lord's point of view. But this monolinguism brought out in man a certain hubris, and with that, a desire to build a tower "whose top may reach unto heaven." The Lord, sensing things would soon get out of hand, decided to "confound their language, that they may not understand one another's speech." Unable to comprehend one another any more, the people abandoned the Tower of Babel.

I love English—I worship it—but I don't want it to be omnipotent. I don't want to return to the time when the whole earth was of one language. Or, rather, to see a day soon when that will be the case. I don't want English to eradicate other tongues. We need to preserve all the world's great, complex, unique linguistic music. Cultures depend on it.

5

The Nerve of Poetry

Have a listen to this story of mine.

I was walking the fields of my farm the other day when, suddenly, I had a thought. It almost seems as if the earth doesn't want there to be barriers between people. Did you ever notice how some stone walls in winter are dislodged by the earth? When it freezes, the earth expands, and that expanding force will often cause certain portions of a stone wall to tumble over. Sometimes the earth's swelling is so pronounced that it will cause quite a few stones to fall and leave a large gap in a wall. I'm not speaking of the holes hunters purposely make. When their dogs think they smell a rabbit there, they'll pull away stone after stone. No, I mean those gaps that just seem to appear out of nowhere. No one ever seems to see them created.

The other day, I had to call my neighbor to walk our property line together to put back these stones. Down the line we went, putting the stones back up on the wall, one by one. Some were small, some bigger. Some wobbled on top, and we had to cast a pretend-spell on them so they would stay balanced. After a while, our hands were calloused from handling so many stones. We came to a space in the land where there is actually no reason to have a wall, or a barrier of any kind. I've got an apple orchard on my land, and he's got pine trees on his. It's not as if my apple trees need to be prevented from eating his pine cones. Why have a wall at all? Neither of us have cows that could wander over to the other's land. I asked him about this, and he said,

"If we have a fence between us, why, there will never be any disputes between us."

Here's how Robert Frost put it:

Mending Wall

Something there is that doesn't love a wall,
That sends the frozen-ground-swell under it,
And spills the upper boulders in the sun;
And makes gaps even two can pass abreast.
The work of hunters is another thing:
I have come after them and made repair
Where they have left not one stone on a stone,
But they would have the rabbit out of hiding,
To please the yelping dogs. The gaps I mean,
No one has seen them made or heard them made,
But at spring mending-time we find them there.
I let my neighbor know beyond the hill;
And on a day we meet to walk the line
And set the wall between us once again.
We keep the wall between us as we go.
To each the boulders that have fallen to each.
And some are loaves and some so nearly balls
We have to use a spell to make them balance:
'Stay where you are until our backs are turned!'
We wear our fingers rough with handling them.
Oh, just another kind of outdoor game,
One on a side. It comes to little more:
There where it is we do not need the wall:
He is all pine and I am apple orchard.
My apple trees will never get across
And eat the cones under his pines, I tell him.
He only says, 'Good fences make good neighbors.'
Spring is the mischief in me, and I wonder
If I could put a notion in his head:
'*Why* do they make good neighbors? Isn't it
Where there are cows? But here there are no cows.
Before I built a wall I'd ask to know
What I was walling in or walling out,
And to whom I was like to give offence.
Something there is that doesn't love a wall,
That wants it down.' I could say 'Elves' to him,
But it's not elves exactly, and I'd rather
He said it for himself. I see him there
Bringing a stone grasped firmly by the top
In each hand, like an old-stone savage armed.
He moves in darkness as it seems to me,
Not of woods only and the shade of trees.
He will not go behind his father's saying,
And he likes having thought of it so well
He says again, 'Good fences make good neighbors.'

So, why did he do that? Why did Robert Frost write this story as a poem? What's in it for us? What can only be communicated in poetry, or communicated far better than in prose?

"Mending Wall" is from Robert Frost's second book, *North of Boston*, published in 1914 in London. (Frost was living in England at the time.) It's the first poem in the collection. The poem is forty-five lines of un-rhymed iambic pentameter and has become famous for the concluding line, "Good fences make good neighbors." The poem is a whole lot more than that. In an interview with the *Paris Review* in 1960 (when Frost was eighty-six), the interviewer summarizes the poet Karl Shapiro who said, "modern poetry is obscure and over difficult…but that isn't true of you [i.e., Frost]." Frost replied, "Well, I don't want to be difficult. I like to fool—oh, you know, you like to be mischievous. But not in that dull way of just being dogged and doggedly obscure."

Then the interviewer pointed out something quite interesting: "The difficulty of your poetry is perhaps in your emphasis on variety in tones of voice."

So, when dealing with Frost, we are dealing with a poet who does not want to be obscure or difficult but who will play with us, who will sing in different voices. Now, whereas there is music in prose, poetry *is* music. So, with that in mind we turn to the first lines of "Mending Wall."

"Something there is that doesn't love a wall" is not a good prose sentence (if you were to end it there). It has a musty, slightly tortured, nineteenth-century feel to it. But it is a singularly memorable and satis-fying line of poetry. The same can be said for the beginning of Frost's "Stopping by Woods on a Snowy Evening": "Whose woods these are I think I know." If this were prose, we might wince. We might even have the urge to rewrite the line to something like, "I think I know who owns these woods." But, as poetry—very different.

So, why torture these poor words like that? Frost does this for several reasons, but first and foremost, I believe, is for the music, for the song. There is a lilting tune here, combined with the lyrics—i.e., the words—that is so seductive. Every good poem is about melody, about music, and in fact this leads to a profound truth about poems and poetry. Seamus Heaney put it well. He said that in lyric poetry, "truthfulness becomes recognizable as a ring of truth within the medium itself." In other words, to alter Keats's line for our purposes, "Truth is Music, Music, Truth."

So, in that first line, Frost gives us:

Some*thing* there *is* that *does*n't *love* a *wall.*

Which is very easy to hum in our head. So, when we read the first line of "Mending Wall," we are reading music. *And we like Frost's tune*, above all. But let's look at the first word, "Something." This is the hero, the subject of the first line, or the culprit, depending on how you look at it. It's vague and mysterious. Even Frost doesn't know who "something" is. (Though later he playfully suggests it might be elves.) And what does he mean, "doesn't love a wall"? How can a "thing" not love anything—much less a wall? Frost is if anything a curious poet, and that curiosity is infectious.

We go on to the second line, then, because we like Frost's music and would like to hear some more of it. And because we're curious. The second line, "That sends the frozen-ground-swell under it," has some miracles in it. The hyphen-connected phrase, "frozen-ground-swell" *looks* like a kind of wave itself, mimics the rising tidal earth. So, because of the hyphens, we get that rolling sensation of the up-pushing earth. Then that mischievous, clever Robert Frost places the phrase "under it" literally *under* the word "wall" from the previous line, thus:

> a wall,
> under it,

So the concept "under" is *actually* under the wall. We see the thing itself happening in a kind of verbal pictogram.

How do you do that in prose?

As readers of poetry we know a lot more than we think we do. Our bodies know the Frost lines are appealing, and no critic or professor has to tell us that. It goes inside us, this pleasure. Every poem is a kind of lullaby in the sense that it harkens back to that time in our lives when music soothed us. However, the music of poetry has changed. Poetry's music—its harmonics and its tunefulness—has changed as much as that of actual music's. Sometimes we like what we hear, sometimes we don't. But we do know with Frost's "Mending Wall,"—quite traditional music—as Seamus Heaney puts it, that we feel "repose in the stability conferred by a musically satisfying order of sounds." Heaney, by the way, loved, as a young poet, the "farmer's accuracy" of Robert Frost and his "wily down-to-earthness," both of which we can see very well in "Mending Wall."

Again the question is: How does poetry have the nerve to be—poetry? How does it have the nerve to look and act the way it does, with its odd shapes, bizarre language, unfathomable ideas, complete unpredictability and general incomprehensibility? How does it have the nerve to create books with titles like, *Tracheal Centrifuge*, *The Stupefying Flashbulbs, Bone Strings* and *Fish De Jour*—all actual recently published titles—and ask us to read them? How does it have the nerve to ask us to wade through all the contortions and obscurities? How does it have the nerve to just lie there, without so much a helping hand, with a look of smug satisfaction on its face, as if to say, "Go ahead—just try to understand me"?

We turn to Philip Larkin for answers. Larkin (1922-1985), was an English poet who worked as a librarian most of his adult life. His poetry often demonstrates Seamus Heaney's thought that "Poetic form is both the ship and the anchor," and one of Larkin's poems in particular, "Talking in Bed," shows what poetry can do so well that prose simply cannot. Poetry, by the fact that it is an extreme distillation in vocabulary and form, focuses us to an extent as we can never be focused in prose. Prose will occasionally focus us with the certainty of poetry, but only rarely. Poems tell stories or focus emotions with such laser-like precision that it's as if we've fallen into a black hole and everything is so dense we can hardly stand it. Here's the Larkin poem:

Talking in Bed

Talking in bed ought to be easiest,
Lying together there goes back so far,
An emblem of two people being honest.

Yet more and more time passes silently.
Outside, the wind's incomplete unrest
Builds and disperses clouds in the sky,

And dark towns heap up on the horizon.
None of this cares for us. Nothing shows why
At this unique distance from isolation

It becomes still more difficult to find
Words at once true and kind,
Or not untrue and not unkind.

Not everything is easy to understand in this poem, but some things are painfully apparent. This is the poet's hand in evidence. We see and we hear a few things right away that we do not have to ponder. Our body tells us so. The poem is brief, a mere twelve lines, and each of those lines is, in itself, brief. The poem is rather lonely-looking there on the page, small and vulnerable. (You can't create that impression with prose.) We feel a kind of subliminal tenderness toward it, wondering if it can stand up for itself, wondering if we even can call it a poem. But indeed it is a poem, and we know poems can be short, because in that respect, poetry's rules are very open-ended. A poem can be extremely short, like Ezra Pound's "In a Station of the Metro":

> The apparition of these faces in the crowd;
> Petals on a wet, black bough.

Or it can go on to the book-length of the *Odyssey*. So, the effect of this brevity—and again I think these are things we don't necessarily verbalize even to ourselves—is that there isn't a lot to say. That there won't be a lot of talking in bed. That these people in fact don't really talk in bed, or, at least, don't talk freely. The poem's language is stark, and its images are as well: "time passes silently," "the wind's incomplete unrest," "None of this cares for us," and "isolation." Ideas and thoughts are conveyed indirectly, "incomplete unrest," "not untrue and not unkind." Communication is strained and painful in every aspect of this poem. It's also marked by absences: There are no names of people. No affection. No kisses. No pillows. No sheets. No lamps. No books. No bodies. Just sadness. Just the not knowing.

Here Larkin is showing us a sad portrait, not to say: "Ah-ha, I know your marriage is dead, and there is no love between you two." But: "How hard it is to be human!" And also: "There, there. I know." He does this with shape and music and by his choice of words and by absence, one of the great advantages of poetry. That is, because a poem is so starkly there, on the page, naked in all that white space, and so brief, many things can be put into focus—including that of the absence of something. We leave "Talking in Bed," with a far longer resonance inside us than the actual length of the poem itself.

This leads us to another fundamental aspect of poetry, a fundamental difference between poetry and prose—shape. Not form, so much, but the actual physical shape of a poem. It's important, because it's often so prominent. A poem not only sounds different than prose, it looks different than prose. Some poems can actually be identified by their shape. You can identify a sonnet by its shape as easily as you can identify certain animals—a pelican, a cat—by their shape. Keats' odes can be picked out of a lineup of variously shaped poems. We know those Odes partially by their shape. Poetry, then, is much more visual than prose. There is a kind of sculptural aesthetic going on, in which shape, physical design, is an important part of the communication. Our ear and our eye are alerted in reading a poem. If we don't read poetry consistently, we are not used to this. This is one reason why poetry can seem foreign to us. But if we can regard a poem with some of the same pleasure and wonder as we do a statue, something three-dimensional, this may help us adjust.

We can't read or hear poetry with the rules of prose. We need to think of it like that profound underwater singing of whales that we cannot hear walking on dry land. This is music that we now know is meant for communication, meant for another world. Just because we can't hear it when we walk around on the earth, doesn't mean it isn't there in all its low-pitched glory. Yet, when we do hear it, when we listen to the recordings that have been made, we are moved by its heroic effort to reach over hundreds of miles of murky, thick, frigid resistant ocean to another whale. We are moved in much the same way by the idea of the great thumping of the elephant's foot, shaking the land to send waves of greeting or sorrow or longing through the earth to a fellow elephant miles away, and unseen, crossing all barriers and entering its foot and body. Poetry enters us in much the same way, whether we realize it or not.

The range of poetry is limitless. There is for every situation a poem, or a poem in waiting, from a child dying to a bird walking on the sand to a note of gratitude to the clothes we wear. I mean fully formed, meaningful, and essential poems that enlighten us, soothe us, or excite us, and confirm "that our very solitudes and distresses are credible," as Heaney says.

Poetry also has a tremendous power that I think many of us saw after September 11. Again, I want to turn to Seamus Heaney, who has so many brilliant things to say about poetry: "There are times when we want the poem not only pleasurably right but compellingly wise, not only a surprising variation played upon the world, but a re-tuning of the world itself. We want the surprise to be transitive like…the electric shock which sets the fibrillating heart back to its proper rhythm." That's what poetry provided to so many of us after September 11. We were dying on the table, and poets set our hearts right again. Or at least they—the old poets—did their best. And they did that I believe partially because poets are determined seekers of truth. Yeats did that for Ireland after the Easter Rebellion when he wrote "Easter 1916" with its widely-quoted line, "A terrible beauty is born." Since no poets have written for us yet great soothing, re-tuning verse about September 11—and I'm not sure why—we have to turn to Yeats and to Whitman and to Auden (his "September 1, 1939" flew all over the Internet after the disaster) and others for our aid.

It was Philip Larkin who wrote that "readability is to a great extent credibility." The title of Seamus Heaney's Nobel Prize lecture, which I have been quoting from so often, is titled, "Crediting Poetry." The credibility of a poet is I think closely tied to morality and to truth, and we "hear" that in the music of the verse. As W.H. Auden wrote in speaking about the poetry of C.P. Cavafy, "Poems made by human beings are no more exempt from moral judgment than acts done by human beings.... One duty of a poem, among others, is to bear witness to the truth." We are attuned to certain voices, and the fact of the matter is that we will be attracted to a poem's music as we will be to a person's character.

A poem feels a bit like an oracle. It feels a bit like someone who appears briefly and speaks the truth, but reveals that truth in metaphors or symbols. The oracles statements were often open to interpretation. Which is why, I believe, some poems have different truths for different readers.

Poems do have character. When we hear or read a poem, part of us is asking, is the poet truthful here? Is he or she courageous? Is the poet being him- or herself? Is he or she sincere? Is he or she compassionate? Does he or she have a sense of pity? Is he or she openhearted? As Theodore Roethke wrote, "Nakedness is my shield." Is he or she sensuous? Funny? In other words, does the poet admit fully and openly his or her humanity? We can see these qualities very clearly in a poet like Wilfred Owen who wrote so bravely and compassionately about the "pity of war" in his poems about World War I. We can see it in Yeats. But this seeking of truth and this open admission of humanity is not always so readily apparent in some of the poems we encounter, which aren't about war or rebellion or death, but about so many other things. But we can hear it. We can hear it if we listen. And a wonderful example of this is the poetry of Elizabeth Bishop.

And so to a poem about a bird walking on the sand. It's called "Sandpiper."

Sandpiper

The roaring alongside he takes for granted,
and that every so often the world is bound to shake.
He runs, he runs to the south, finical, awkward,
in a state of controlled panic, a student of Blake.

The beach hisses like fat. On his left, a sheet
of interrupting water comes and goes
and glazes over his dark and brittle feet.
He runs, he runs straight through it, watching his toes.

—Watching, rather, the spaces of sand between them,
where (no detail too small) the Atlantic drains
rapidly backwards and downwards. As he runs,
he stares at the dragging grains.

The world is a mist. And then the world is
minute and vast and clear. The tide
is higher or lower. He couldn't tell you which.
His beak is focussed; he is preoccupied,

looking for something, something, something.
Poor bird, he is obsessed!
The millions of grains are black, white, tan, and gray,
mixed with quartz grains, rose and amethyst.

From the very first line, we trust the poet completely. Why? When we read, "The roaring alongside he takes for granted," we sense wit, a keen eye, imagination, and sympathy. We sense the fact that we're welcomed. We do not feel exclusion as we do with some poets. This is because Bishop is saying, "You're savvy enough, you're curious enough, to know I don't have to point out that "roaring" refers to the ocean's noise." (We already know, from the title, it's about a bird that feeds near the ocean.) That's *inclusive*. She also is saying to us that, "I think you'll enjoy the fact that I'm going to instantly put him in action on the wet sand doing his sandpiper thing, and so you know what I mean when I say, 'alongside.'" This is focus, with fun. This is what poetry can do, it can focus your eye, like the prison searchlight on the escaping criminal. So Bishop is saying, you're easily as smart as I am, so I want to show you this picture I've drawn. I've left out some of the dots, but the fun of it is that I know you can fill them in and will like filling them in yourself.

I think her most smile-inducing phrase of this kind in the poem is the first line of the second stanza, "The beach hisses like fat." This line is actually half written by the reader. When Bishop writes "like fat," we instantly know she means fat in a frying pan being cooked. It's the leaving the pan and fire out that makes the line thrilling, not the least of which we see that it *can* be left out. The second brilliance is that it's the beach that hisses, not the ocean. Our minds most likely think of the ocean making the noise in its withdrawal, but it's the beach that hisses after the ocean's leaving. I don't think prose can provide us with this powerful sense of arm-in-arm between writer and reader as poetry can, and on such a consistent basis.

Elizabeth Bishop was actually a fine drawer of real pictures. One of her delightful watercolors is on the cover of her *Complete Poems*. She draws another welcoming picture in a poem called, "The Shampoo":

The Shampoo

The still explosions on the rocks,
the lichens, grow
by spreading, gray, concentric shocks.
They have arranged
to meet the rings around the moon, although
within our memories they have not changed.

And since the heavens will attend
as long on us,
you've been, dear friend,
precipitate and pragmatical;
and look what happens. For Time is
nothing if not amenable.

The shooting stars in your black hair
in bright formation
are flocking where,
so straight, so soon?
—Come, let me wash it in this big tin basin,
battered and shiny like the moon.

Even before the explanatory second line, "the lichens, grow," you know, with the first line, "The still explosions on the rocks," that you are seeing something new. Or, really, that you knew, but never really saw. One of the oldest, most durable and least dynamic living things, lichens, suddenly become a "still explosion." We see the essence of the lichen's behavior, its concentric expanding circles, and suddenly our mind snaps awake. Now we think of the millennium-moving lichens as having a spreading, tsunami-like quality to them. The poet says, *I can describe this*. And as with any revelation we have through art, somewhere we knew this already. Seamus Heaney loved the "pure consequence of Elizabeth Bishop's style."

So we trust Bishop completely. Our mind has fallen in love. And we do the same with Pablo Neruda and his *Odas Elementales*, Elemental Odes. Now we come to the poem of gratitude for the clothes we wear. It's called "Oda al Traje," Ode to the Clothes. Yes, it's a translation we're discussing here of the great Chilean poet's verse, but we are less concerned with Neruda's music than with his welcoming, and with his heart. It begins,

Ode to the Clothes

Every morning you wait,
clothes, over a chair,
for my vanity,
my love,
my hope, my body
to fill you,

In these first lines, we feel sweetness, sympathy, humanity and perhaps above all, mortality. We know there will be a time when the poet will be gone—as he in fact is—and will not put himself in these clothes. Are we not more than willing to put ourselves in the hands of this poet who honors his everyday clothes? I think with both Bishop and Neruda there is also a sense of rectitude that flows through their poems, borne out by this sympathy and openheartedness and compassion. So, as with a person whose character is strong and that we admire, we are better people for having spent time with him or her. So it is with certain poems and poets.

Poetry, because of its heightened condensation and its special music can shock us, too. Prose can hardly approach it in this sense. This will often happen at the close of the poem. Here is an example from the great Greek poet C.P. Cavafy (1863-1933), who spent his life working and writing in Alexandria, Egypt. The poem is called "The City":

The City

You said, "I will go to another land, I will go to another sea.
Another city will be found, a better one than this.
Every effort of mine is a condemnation of fate;
and my heart is—like a corpse—buried.
How long will my mind remain in this wasteland.
Wherever I turn my eyes, wherever I may look
I see black ruins of my life here,
where I spent so many years destroying and wasting."

You will find no new lands, you will find no other seas.
The city will follow you. You will roam the same
streets. And you will age in the same neighborhoods;
and you will grow gray in the same houses.
Always you will arrive in this city. Do not hope for any other—
There is no ship for you, there is no road.
As you have destroyed your life here
in this little corner, you have ruined it in the entire world.

Those last two lines! Truth stares us in the face. This is the honesty and rectitude of a great poet as truth-seeker. I don't know how prose can match poetry's ability to give such a punch to our moral solar plexus so quickly, as demonstrated in these mere sixteen lines. There is no way to escape the poet's gaze, his prison searchlight, in this tightly confined space. We must look ourselves in the eye. If it's painful, well, the great poet will never compromise with the truth. That's something, painful as it may be, we can rely on with the best of our poets and their poetry.

Part 2

Writing

6

Using the Techniques of Fiction to Make Your Creative Nonfiction Even More Creative: Character, Setting, and Drama

A great irony of creative nonfiction is that one of its chief assets is also one of its chief liabilities. This is the fact that in nonfiction everything actually happened. It's all true. One of the reasons we eagerly turn to nonfiction is because we have it on reliable sources—most often, in any case—that the events on the page actually took place and the people who did them were, or are, real. A good part of our astonishment at reading Ernest Shackleton's account of his eight-hundred-mile open boat voyage from Elephant Island across the terrible frigid sea to South Georgia Island, for example, is that real men went through this, with real fears and real hopes, who had real families at home and real men left behind cold and hungry depending on their success. This *happened.*

This is what makes the book, *Alive: The Story of the Andes Survivors,* so strong, as well. The story of an airplane crashing in the Andes and the survivors resorting to eating the flesh of their dead comrades in order to survive moves us deeply. Real people, not so unlike us, went through that experience. Who is to say that one day something like that might happen to one of us? We wonder how we might act. If this were in a novel, we might easily dismiss it, and it probably wouldn't plague our hearts and minds with sympathy and horror in so intimate a way as it does in *Alive.*

But the cold clear fact is that no matter how astonishing the story, there is no guarantee that it will be interesting writing. Many writers of nonfiction, particularly in the ever-burgeoning category of memoir, seem to believe the strength of their subject is enough to keep the reader captivated. After all, if you slept with your mother, or father, or both, and your dog, shouldn't that be sufficient to keep the reader turning the pages? More seriously, the stories of memoir, and of nonfiction in general, are often desperately sad, even tragic—and in some cases, as with Ernest Shackleton's, heroic—and so writers, under the sway of the powerful emotions associated with those events, often feel that simply by spilling out those events on the page, like the contents of a toolbox, the reader will experience these emotions as clearly and strongly as the writer.

Not so. Or, often enough, not so. So, the fact that something actually happened is both the boon and the bane of creative nonfiction. It's a terrific asset, because so many of the things that happen in real life would just not be plausible in fiction. How many times have we heard someone say, "If this were an idea for a novel, it would be laughable. But it *really happened*." The great historical novelist Patrick O'Brian said, in speaking of the exploits of the Royal Navy of the eighteenth century, "So very often the improbable reality outruns fiction." So, you can tell those implausible stories in nonfiction, because, by the very nature of the genre, they did indeed happen. However, the fact of a crash in the Andes, or a climb up Everest, or a battle against cancer, or living under a cruel and repressive government, is not enough to make the *writing* good. In too many cases, the subject matter can work against the writer. It can lull the writer into a false sense of literary security.

Here's something else: The fact that the characters in the story are, or were, actually alive can be an inhibitor to good prose. Especially when these characters are well known—and often related—to the writer. They are quite embedded in the writer's consciousness, and exist in a kind of shorthand in his or her mind. Invented characters do not, because the writer has to start from scratch. They are built brick by brick, as it were, gesture by gesture, opinion by opinion, act by act, strand of hair by strand of hair, so that they are almost as fresh to the to the reader as they are to the writer.

In the case of Caddy in *The Sound and the Fury,* for instance, it began with Faulkner seeing in his mind's eye a picture of the young girl's muddy drawers as she climbed a tree. He built his character from there. In other words, the reader, in one sense, knows the characters nearly as well, or for nearly as long, as the writer. That is not the case with nonfiction characters. The writer often knows them much better than the reader ever will. The reader doesn't know them at all, to begin with, while the writer may have been living with them for years, either literally—or figuratively, through research. So there can be an enormous gap between reader and writer. If the writer isn't conscious of this gap, then he or she can leave the reader behind, looking at a shell of a character and wondering where the rest of the body is.

Think of your conversations with your siblings or parents about a relative or a close friend. You don't have to explain anything to each other. If, for example, you have an uncle who likes to steal ashtrays at social occasions, you don't have to say, "Well, you know how Berty likes to steal ashtrays at parties." If you did, you'd be telling the other person something he or she already knows, and it would be more of a conversation opener than anything else. You could just declare, "Well, Berty took another one. And this time he really outdid himself." This common accrued knowledge allows for a kind of emotional code, or shorthand. Sometimes nonfiction writers write this way, as if their readers know a lot more about the character, or characters, than they actually do. They can be far too assuming. It may be unintended assuming, or subconscious assuming, but it is assuming nevertheless.

So, the nonfiction writer must step back and consider his or her characters as strangers. He or she must introduce them to the reader, as if the character or characters stepped out of a novel, or out of thin air, as it were. This can be difficult. How do you look at your father, your mother, your husband, your children as strangers? Well, you can. And you must. It's imperative to make your characters—and this seems quite paradoxical—as real as any fictional characters. They must be built from the ground up.

You can do that with the help of the techniques of fiction, and by being continually aware of the need to make them real.

These same commitments to achieving the realism fictional characters possess apply as well to other aspects of fiction—to setting the scene; to creating a sense of drama; to choosing the exact word; to creating a kind of music, or melody, in your nonfiction prose; in fact, to all the subtleties of fine fiction. This chapter aims to point out some of these areas and to demonstrate, with examples from the world of fiction, how your nonfiction writing can become more dynamic. In short, how it can have the advantages of nonfiction with the proven techniques of fiction. The fact is, many nonfiction writers I've taught are often mystified why their story isn't as well received as they think it should be. "But…it's such a tragic story! It's so full of pain and sorrow!" Yes, for *you*. Now, you have to make the reader feel that as well. That's a different story.

It all begins with character. Character is at the heart of any story. We remember books by their characters. In very rare cases, as with Ivan Turgenev, we may remember the landscape as fixedly as the characters, but there are not many writers with the sensitivity and deep connection to nature—not to mention genius—as he. We *remember* Don Quixote,

David Copperfield, Robinson Crusoe, Huck Finn, Jay Gatsby, Nathan Zuckerman, and so on. The question, for the nonfiction writer, is how, and why.

Often the most important character of all in nonfiction is the narrator, especially in memoir. The narrator, of course, is you. But you as a *character.* Some writings recently have taken pains to demonstrate why and how you, as the writer, need to separate yourself from your basic everyday ego and to mold yourself into a character. One fine example is Vivian Gornick's *The Situation and the Story: The Art of Personal Narrative.* It's *difficult* having this ego tied to us, to borrow from Yeats, "as to a dog's tail." I think it's a good idea to distance yourself from you ego—as a character, I mean—as much as possible. You need your ego, naturally, to write. The ego provides all that confidence you require to justify putting pen to paper. But when your self lacks perspective and humility, then you, the narrator, can become overwhelming, if not downright boorish at times. So, how do you keep yourself a respectable character who doesn't chew the scenery or simply become too overbearing—a kind of tyrant in ink?

There's no better example than *The Great Gatsby.* It's written in the first person—but what a sweet, somewhat diffident, wonder-filled narrator Nick Carraway is. From the opening lines where Nick harkens back to some words of wisdom from his father, the tone is set:

> In my younger and more vulnerable years my father gave me some advice that I've been turning over in my mind ever since. "Whenever you feel like criticizing any one," he told me, "just remember that all the people in this world haven't had the advantages that you've had."

And shortly after, Nick says, "In consequence, I'm inclined to reserve all judgments, a habit that has opened up many curious natures to me and also made me the victim of not a few veteran bores."

So, right away we know we're dealing with a sympathetic nature. We're dealing with someone whom people confide in. We all know these kinds of people. We feel safe with them. They aren't going to judge us. That doesn't make them any less intelligent or perceptive. It just means they have a generous heart. This is Nick Carraway, the man—the narrator—with whom we are going to pass several hundred pages. And we are most pleased to be in his company. Now, can we say Fitzgerald was Carraway? Not really. They may have things in common—an obsessive, worshipful curiosity about wealth, perhaps. But Nick Carraway must be separate from Fitzgerald; he will live forever, and he must perform his job each and every time a reader picks up *The Great Gatsby.*

Nick is an excellent role model, as far as narrators go. The traits of diffidence, courtesy, sympathy, and a sense of wonder can go a long way toward creating a narrator that is likeable and effective. Your story may require a tougher narrator—the Dorothy Allison of *Skin: Talking About Sex, Class and Literature,* for example. But I think you will notice that her narrator is still extremely vulnerable. So you may be able to have both. The idea is to look at *Gatsby,* at its narrator, and see what you can use in developing your own narrator.

As a narrator, you certainly want to distance yourself from self-pity, that most lethal of emotions, especially if you are telling a pitiful story. You can look to *The Catcher in the Rye* for a good lesson on how to avoid that. This is a novel about that inherently dangerous field mined with self-pity—adolescence. How does the first-person narrator, Holden Caulfield, save us from a roomful of hand-wringing angst?

With humor. With the sub-category of lacerating sarcasm, much of it directed at himself. We remember, for instance, Holden pledges that he won't try to kiss or fondle any girl he doesn't like:

> I keep making up these sex rules for myself, and then I break them right away. Last year I made a rule that I was going to quit horsing around with girls that, deep down, gave me a pain in the ass. I broke it, though, the same week I made it—the same *night* as a matter of fact.

This kind of wry confession can go a long way toward endearing the reader to the writer, particularly in trying circumstances. Hardly anything is so serious as to preclude humor. If you don't think so, then pick up a copy of Art Spiegelman's *Maus,* that incredible graphic novel about the Holocaust. Full as it is of great pity and compassion, it also has its share of humor, much of it at the narrator's expense. It's also a good book to examine to see how Spiegelman distanced himself from himself—in this case, with a mask of a mouse over his face. Though he is so wry as to make himself visible to us beneath the mask. It's not a very good mask. So there is both tenderness at his obviousness and wryness, as well.

I think it might be a good exercise to think of yourself, to think of your narrator, with a large dollop of self-deprecation. Not to take yourself so seriously. Pick out a fault of yours, or a mistake. Make it obvious to the reader. Make yourself human. Omniscient, perhaps, but not omnipotent.

A third way a writer can make us feel sympathetic toward his or her narrator in nonfiction is with honesty, with truthfulness. This isn't about facts. This is about nakedness. This is not about being selectively confessional—and aren't all confessions selective? This is about standing nude before the reader. To see that, you need just to turn to the work of Jean Rhys. She is an amazing writer, she defies category, and I'm sure she must confound critics by being so uncontritely miserable. Many of her books are about self-degradation and humiliation, but God she can write! This is from *Good Morning, Midnight:*

> On the contrary, it's when I am quite sane like this, when I have a couple of extra drinks and am quite sane, that I realize how lucky I am. Saved, rescued, fished-up, half-drowned, out of the deep, dark river, dry clothes, hair shampooed and set. Nobody would know I had ever been in it. Except, of course, that there always remains something. Yes, there always remains something…. Never mind, here I am, sane and dry, with my place to hide in. What more do I want?… I'm a bit of an automaton, but sane, surely—dry, cold and sane. Now I have forgotten about dark streets, dark rivers, the pain, the struggle and the drowning…. Mind you, I'm not talking about the struggle when you are strong and a good swimmer and there are willing and eager friends on the bank waiting to pull you out at the first sign of distress. I mean the real thing. You jump in with no willing and eager friends around, and when you sink you sink to the accompaniment of loud laughter.

If that doesn't put a shiver down your spine, I'm not sure what will. It also has another effect on the reader—one of deep sympathy for this writer's bravery. I think the idea is to be less protective of yourself as narrator. Vivian Gornick does an admirable job of this in her memoir, *Fierce Attachments.* This is not a woman who is at peace with herself, and perhaps may not even like herself. You trust this narrator, because she doesn't hide. I say this even in the face of the fact that Gornick has stated that she "composed" some scenes—that is, combined several events into one—in this book. I can disassociate this act of the *writer,* and its controversy, from the narrator.

Now, let's turn to characters *other* than the narrator: To your characters in your story. Character in fiction is defined, basically, in five ways: By what a person says or thinks; by the dialogue that person has with other characters; by what a person does; by what others say about that person; and by the physical description of that person. There are likely more methods, but these seem to me sufficient, at least to begin with. Here's how Joseph Conrad shows us his Lord Jim for the first time:

> He was an inch, perhaps two, under six feet, powerfully built, and he advanced straight at you with a slight stoop of the shoulders, head forward, and a fixed from-under stare which made you think of a charging bull. His voice was deep, loud, and his manner displayed a kind of dogged self-assertion which had nothing aggressive in it. It seemed a necessity, and it was directed apparently as much at himself as at anybody else.

These three sentences bear scrutiny. The details are fascinating, starting with the height, "an inch, perhaps two," which, in its indefiniteness, makes it absolutely precise and indelible. Moreover, there is, in the physical description, a foreshadowing of what we will come to know. The "deep, loud voice" has "nothing aggressive in it" and "was directed apparently as much at himself as at anybody else." This is the man who left hundreds of pilgrims to die on the open water and must live with that decision inside himself for the rest of his life. The aggression is turned inward. His deep, loud voice is meant for him.

Not many of us can write like Conrad; however, that shouldn't preclude us from drawing our nonfiction characters more vividly. Conrad is a good model for us in that effort. There's no reason at all you can't describe your grandfather or brother or uncle with more dramatic precision by simply paying very close attention to how they walk, talk, sit, run, eat, etc. In fact, there may even be a way to link this to an aspect of their personality, Lord Jim-wise.

As for making a character more three dimensional by showing us how he or she thinks, one of the classic examples of this is Dostoyevsky's *Notes From Underground,* perhaps the most famous rant in literature. A passage which demonstrates the wonderfully bizarre humor of the novella comes toward the end of Part I:

> I'd feel better if I could only believe something of what I've written down here. But I swear I can't believe a single word of it. That is, I believe it in a way, but at the same time, I feel I'm lying like a son of a bitch.
> "Then why have you written all this?" you may ask.
> Well, I wish I could stick you into a mousehole for forty years or so with nothing to do, and at the end of that time I'd like to see what kind of state you'd be in.

Too true. And what are we to believe at this point?

Of course, the master of the interior monologue was Shakespeare, but we'll leave the Bard and his fellow dramatists alone and stay with our writers of fiction.

In a variation on this, you can demonstrate qualities of your character by showing your readers letters they have written. This has been done in fiction consistently. There is an entire genre devoted to this. In nonfiction, Russell Baker uses this technique ably by quoting from a series of poignant letters from a suitor of his mother's in his book, *Growing Up.* The letters were written during the Depression, and finally, at a certain point, the writer, a man whose English is not perfect—and this makes the letters even more touching—simply is swallowed up by the hard times, and disappears. His letters reveal matters of the heart that even the surest writer couldn't capture. Letters are often available to memoirists. They can make a strong addition to a story and show us more of who that person really is you're trying to tell us about.

Now, how about the idea of making a character stronger on the page by showing what people say about him or her? I think of Charles Dickens' *A Christmas Carol*. We all remember when the spirit of Christmas to come takes Scrooge to a conversation between two men who are speaking about Scrooge himself. Scrooge doesn't realize who they are talking about as he eavesdrops, and the men say things none too kind about him. Then, of course, he realizes they are speaking of him *posthumously*. What a literary device that is! Now, you can't have your characters reveal the future, but you can certainly record conversations that other people have about them. An example of an entire book constructed this way is *Edie: American Girl,* edited by Jean Stein and George Plimpton, which is the story of Edie Sedgwick, an Andy Warhol girl, as told by people who knew her. (A movie, *Factory Girl,* was made about her in 2006.) I don't think Edie herself utters a word in the book. It's one of the most effective and original American biographies ever written, and by proxy, as it were. I think especially of people you want to write about who have recently died. There often are others who knew them and are living, and who can speak about them. This is what Laura Hillenbrand found out in writing her book, *Seabiscuit: An American Legend.* The three main characters in her book had passed away, but there were plenty of people who knew them, and who had seen the great Seabiscuit race. Her greatest source, Hillenbrand has said about her book, was living memory.

We can again turn to Conrad for an instance of drawing a character by what other people say about him—to *Heart of Darkness* and the infamous Kurtz. As the narrator Marlow's boat edges further and further down the Congo, we hear more and more about the fabled ivory hunter Kurtz—and we hear that wonderful line, "The man has enlarged my mind!" uttered by one of Kurtz's worshipful minions. His reputation grows more grotesquely huge until Kurtz becomes both a god and a devil in our minds. We know him chiefly by what others say of him, and that makes his legend even larger and more dramatic. When we finally do meet him, he is nothing like his legend. The jungle has made a shadow of him. This is the carefully planned shock Conrad gives us. In *Apocalypse Now*, when Francis Ford Coppola actually shows us his Kurtz in the form of Marlon Brando, I think there is a palpable letdown. He develops Kurtz the same way as Conrad does—by having others speak of him in great and awesome detail. No living being can equal that reputation, and we might be better off, perhaps, never meeting the man.

This technique of building a character by what others say about him or her seems to me quite accessible to writers of any stripe. And quite a good way to create a sense of drama. If, for example, you begin your story with comments and anecdotes about your character told by others, and bide your time before you actually bring this character physically on the stage, you already have a sense of built-in drama and expectation. This was certainly the case with Harry Lime in the 1949 movie, *The Third Man.* The entire film is one fine exercise in anticipation. We hear all about Harry Lime from various characters in the movie's post-World War II Vienna, but we don't in fact actually see him—played with wonderfully cynical aplomb by Orson Welles—until the film is almost two-thirds over. By then, we can hardly wait. The screenwriter, Graham Greene, knew what he was doing.

We can know a character by what he or she does. And for that, look to Henry Miller. As Paul Theroux wrote in an obituary about Miller, he had one subject and that was himself. But he wrote novels, he wrote fiction. He is narrator and main character in most of his books, if not in all. (Even in his critical books. The poet Karl Shapiro said Miller's study of Arthur Rimbaud, *The Time of the Assassins*, is as much about Miller as it is about Rimbaud.) So, here you have a narrator whose actions are doubtful to say the least. In *The Rosy Crucifixion*, his mistreats his wife terribly and abandons his child. He considers his only responsibility to be that toward his own talent. He borrows money from anyone who breathes, fully intending never to pay it back. He glorifies himself in conversation. After a while we get a pretty good picture of the man. The fact that some of us still find him worthy—and I am one of them—is a measure, I think, of other more admirable aspects of his character.

I remember how in Susan Cheever's memoir, *Home Before Dark,* she speaks of how her famous father, the writer John Cheever, was poorly paid by the *New Yorker* and yet chose to remain with the magazine, even in lieu of a much more lucrative offer from I think it was the *Saturday Evening Post.* He had a family to support, and didn't make much money, and so the revelation of this decision carries great weight with the reader. We learn something significant about the man by what he did.

As for dialogue revealing character, a strong example is Hemingway's short story, "A Clean, Well-Lighted Place." This story is set in a café in Spain late at night, near or even past closing time, where two waiters are waiting on an old man to finish his drink so they can close up. But the old man doesn't want to leave. He wants another drink. He likes the café, where he feels comfortable, and can maintain a sense of dignity. Most of the story is a dialogue between the two waiters about the old man. What we learn, just by what the men say, is that the two waiters are very different. One is ultimately sympathetic toward the old man, and the other is not. Hemingway constructs the dialogue in such a way as to show us the lack of sympathy in one waiter and the tenderness and compassion in the other. All with conversation. So, let your nonfiction characters develop on the page with dialogue. Their words will reveal themselves.

Nonfiction has done a much better job in terms of setting the scene, I think. This probably has a lot to do with the fact that so much of it takes place outside—or in houses or cabins or tents in or near the wilderness. Think of all the splendid nature writing, and adventure writing—from Thoreau to Muir to Dillard, from Shackleton to Saint-Exupéry, where we have fine settings of scenes. I think memoirists need pay heed here. Setting the scene precisely and well is too often overlooked in memoir. I'm not sure exactly why. But we—the readers—want to be *grounded.* We want to know where we are. What kind of world we're in. Not only that, it is so often the case in nonfiction that the scene itself is a kind of character. Take the Kansas of Truman Capote's *In Cold Blood,* for example. Capote takes pains right at the beginning of his book to set the scene of his multiple murders on the plains and wheat fields of the Midwest. I think the movies of his book were influenced by this emphasis, as well.

Photography can help here, as well. If you look once again at the astonishing photographs Walker Evans took as part of what would become *Let Us Now Praise Famous Men* by James Agee, you will have a memorable lesson. The people are heartbreaking, yes, and some will stay with you until the day you die. But look at the *setting,* look at the scene, look at the black and white photographs of the houses and the rooms and the porches these people lived in. Look at their beds, at their chairs, tables, walls. That is in many ways as heartbreaking as the people themselves. *They* tell a story. There is one photograph in particular that has seared itself into my heart. It's a simple shot of the inside wall of one of the sharecropper's houses. The wall is probably pine, rough-hewn, unpainted and unvarnished. There is a small piece of wood nailed against it, leaving a space where the owner has crookedly put seven or eight knives and forks. This is all you need to know about how they live. Sometimes, presenting a life indirectly is the most effective way.

Nonfiction writers should show the reader where the story takes place, and in vivid detail. John Knowles' *A Separate Peace* is an example how of one can set a scene. Here's how that novel begins,

> I went back to the Devon School not long ago, and found it looking oddly newer than when I was a student there fifteen years before. It seemed more sedate than I remembered it, more perpendicular and straight-laced, with narrower windows and shinier woodwork, as though a coat of varnish had been put on everything for better preservation. But, of course, fifteen years before there had been a war going on. Perhaps the school wasn't as well kept up in those days; perhaps varnish, along with everything else, had gone to war.

This not an especially dramatic opening; in fact, it's very calm, and easy. What one notices, though, is the soft personification of the school. It is "more sedate," and "straight-laced." Right away, the school is being likened to a person, perhaps to a typical boarding school teacher, who knows? I think the point here is that this kind of method can be applied to any place, to any building, to any store, and so on. When I spoke to some students recently about setting, I asked them to describe the building we were all in—which happened to be an old wooden church—as a person. They were to do this in the form of a metaphor, not a simile; in other words, the building *was* the person, or vice-versa. Any nonfiction writer can employ this method in describing the house they grew up in, or the school he or she attended. It gives more bounce to the prose. It makes it stronger.

Let's compare this to the beginning of *Guard of Honor* by James Gould Cozzens, an author best known for his book, *By Love Possessed*. *Guard of Honor* is a fine book, and you will often see it on "Neglected Novels" lists that are compiled every once in a while. Here is its beginning and scene setting:

> Through the late afternoon they flew southeast, going home to Ocanara at about two hundred miles an hour. Inside the spic and span fuselage—the plane was a new twin-engine advanced trainer of the type designated AT-7—this speed was not noticeable. Though the engines steadily and powerfully vibrated and time was passing, the shining plane seemed stationary, swaying gently and slightly oscillating, a little higher than the stationary, dull-crimson sphere of the low sun. It hung at perpetual dead center in an immense shallow bowl of summer haze, delicately lavender. The bottom of the bowl, six thousand feet below, was colored a soft olive brown; a blending, hardly distinguishable, of the wide, swampy river courses, the overgrown hammocks, the rolling, heat-shaken savannas, the dry, trackless, palmetto flatlands that make up so much of the rank but poor champaign of lower Alabama and northwestern Florida. Within the last few minutes, far off and too gradually to break the illusion of standing still, the dim, irregular edge of an enormous, flat, metallic-gray splotch had begin to appear. It was the Gulf of Mexico.

Aside from the extended alliteration, most of it with "s's," and quite surprisingly successful, one can find in this long paragraph some good ideas for setting the scene. Now, granted, the scene is being painted from a perspective far above, but just look at the wonderful "enormous, flat, metallic-gray splotch" that is the Gulf of Mexico. A splotch! The idea that you can transform an enormous body of water into a mere splotch is not just an act of creativity, but a leap of faith. You have to be more than simply creative, you have to be bold. You have to trust yourself. Somewhere inside, you are telling yourself, well, it looks like a splotch, like some ink I spilt. Perhaps another part of you is saying, don't be absurd, this is a gigantic body of water, you can't call it a splotch. Cozzens listened to the right voice, and we, his readers, benefit from his courage. Let this be a lesson for our nonfiction.

Now we come to drama.

We writers all want it. We all need it. We want our readers to be thrilled, excited, moved, and, most of all, *not* bored. In creative nonfiction, we need drama at least as much as in fiction. That's because, to return to the opening premise of this chapter, the subject matters for nonfiction, and especially memoir, are inherently dramatic—dying of cancer, being molested, falling off a mountain—but the writer may too often decide the fact these things actually happened is sufficient drama in itself. That can be a fatal mistake. The question is how can we take these events and produce a drama that extends far beyond ourselves to the rest of the unknown world.

Drama comes in all shapes and sizes. I believe drama is best produced quietly, rather than by shouting or by weeping and wailing. It often takes a while to produce. There is a memorable example in a Sherwood Anderson short story, "Adventure," from *Winesburg, Ohio*. The main character, Alice Hindman, makes love with a young man one reckless evening, only to have him leave for Chicago to seek his fortune. He promises to return, or to send for her, and then they will be married. But he never does. Still, she keeps waiting through the years. Her behavior becomes more and more erratic. Finally, one stormy evening, "a strange desire took possession of her," and she undresses and runs naked out of the house into the rain. A drunken old man wandering by sees her:

> Alice dropped to the ground and lay trembling. She was so frightened at the thought of what she had done that when the man had gone on his way she did not dare get to her feet, but crawled on hands and knees through the grass to the house. When she got to her own room she bolted the door and drew her dressing table across the doorway. Her body shook as with a chill and her hands trembled so that she had dif-

ficulty getting into her night-dress. When she got into bed she buried her face in the pillow and wept brokenheartedly. "What is the matter with me? I will do something dreadful if I am not careful," she thought, and turning her face to the wall, began trying to force herself to face bravely the fact that many people must live and die alone, even in Winesburg.

That last sentence! It explodes with drama, quietly on the page, but hugely in our hearts, because of all the dashed hopes and delusions that have preceded it, step by quiet step. Anderson is a master at telling a story simply and surely.

The opening line of your story can have as much drama as the last line. I don't mean to suggest that every story you write need have a dramatic opening line and ending line, but, well, that wouldn't be bad, either. Your first line should, though, capture the reader's attention and force him or her to read onward. This can be accomplished by making it a kind of ultra-condensed piece of information. Take the beginning of Stephen Crane's "The Open Boat:" "None of them knew the color of the sky." We understand, from the title of the story, that there is an open boat. We infer the said open boat is on the sea, or on some large body of water. We also infer there are people in it. So, when we are given the information that none of them knew the color of the sky, we also infer, and rightly, because the sentence is so precisely constructed, that they are too weary to raise their heads to determine the color of the sky. So, ultimately, we conclude that they have been in this open boat for a long time, which is exactly what Crane wants us to conclude. All done with a mere nine words.

One more example of the calm before the storm—again, from *In Cold Blood*. At one point Truman Capote is relating the killer Perry Smith's account of the Clutter family murder. Smith is calmly and evenly talking about Herb Clutter, the father. Up to thus point, we know Smith is the killer, but he's never admitted it. Then, he says, simply, "I didn't want to harm the man. I thought he was a very nice gentleman. Soft-spoken. I thought so right up to the moment I cut his throat." Nothing else, no exclamation marks. No, "Oh my God's!" from Capote. Just that—naked for us to see. Then on to the next paragraph. This seems to me a perfect example of how to convey something horrible (or sad, tragic, miserable) to the reader—calmly and clearly, without editorializing.

Creating drama, then, is often a case of letting the act speak for itself.

Of course, if you do have something really dramatic to reveal, some-times the best way to reveal it is with a big, fat splash. In Sir Arthur Conan

Doyle's *The Hound of the Baskervilles*, Sherlock Holmes is being told the details of the death of Sir Charles Baskerville by his friend and doctor, James Mortimer. This is how Conan Doyle ends Chapter II:

> "'But one false statement was made by Barrymore [the butler] at the inquest. He said that there were no traces upon the ground round the body. He did not observe any. But I did—some little distance off, but fresh and clear.'
> "'Footprints?'
> "'Footprints.'
> "'A man or woman's?'
> "Dr. Mortimer looked strangely at us for an instant and his voice sank almost to a whisper as he answered:
> "'Mr. Holmes, they were the footprints of a gigantic hound!'"

Some things you don't want to leave to the imagination. You don't want to whisper them. There is absolutely nothing wrong about being emphatic when you need to be. Notice, though, how that scene, that entire chapter, builds up to this dramatic revelation, and how it leaves us hanging, almost falling in anticipation. There is no reason why you cannot think specifically of drama when writing nonfiction in the way a fiction writer does, by creating a sense of surprise for the reader, either softly or loudly. This is far more effective than just spilling the events on the page.

The fact that your story is true is a powerful weapon to have on your side. The idea, though, is not to take the writing of it for granted. And for that lesson, there is no better place to turn than to the world of fiction. The very best creative nonfiction writers always have, and you feel that world reverberate through their stories like a bell.

7

Finding a Great Title

The real beginning of your book—or essay, poem, story—is its title. Think about it. The title is the first word or set of words the reader reads. This isn't just a linguistic trick, it's an important distinction. Someone is browsing in a bookstore. What do they see? The cover, of course. They see an illustration or a photograph—and then: the title. This is where they actually begin to *read* your words. The same is true with someone thumbing through a magazine, or an anthology. They come to a story, or to an essay. The first words they read are those in the title. If your title is arresting, it can get them to open the book and to read on. If it isn't, it can lose them, right then and there.

Nance Van Winckel, in her absorbing and meticulously researched essay, "Staking the Claim of the Title," says, "We can't exactly 'read' the title at the outset—i.e. get a sense of its meaning or relevance—because it doesn't yet have enough context to allow for that. So we glance at the title, perhaps muse a split second, then store it away." I see her point, especially when she's referring to titles whose meaning is obscure until you have read the text. (*Jude the Obscure*, for example.) However, I think this is much more the case with poetry—the main focus of Van Winckel's essay—than with creative nonfiction or fiction. Writers of creative nonfiction, for example, are much more likely to affix a revelatory subtitle to their titles.

If you take a title like *The Perfect Storm: A True Story of Men Against The Sea*, it's true that you do not know from just those words that it's a book about swordfishing and men who go down in a swordfishing boat. However, you certainly do know that it will be about one hell of a storm, that it's a true story, and that some sort of big struggle is involved. More than that, though, you already have an idea of the writer's style—concentrated, yet lyrical; simple, easy to comprehend, strong—and his sense of irony. In other words, of what kind of guide and companion you'll have the next few hundred pages. You have begun reading.

From a practical point of view, too, the title is the way your book, or story, is remembered. It's the way the book is spoken about in conversation. It's the way your book is ordered in a bookstore, and, hopefully, re-ordered—and, if you're lucky, nominated for prizes. It should be memorable, don't you think, if you want people to remember it? Sounds simple, but there are many titles that just *aren't* that memorable. Does anyone doubt that the title *Moby-Dick* has been a powerful asset in assuring eternal life for Melville's masterpiece? Short, simple, exotic, and strong, this title of a mere two words and three syllables has become nearly eradicable from our memories.

And tell me, wouldn't you find it hard to resist opening the covers of these books—which is, of course, the point:

Girl, Interrupted; *Autobiography of a Face*; *The Killer Inside Me*; *Fear and Loathing in Las Vegas*; *Sex, Faith, Mystery*; *Dry Guillotine*; *Sailing Alone Around The World*; *They Shoot Horses, Don't They?*; *The Man Who Liked Slow Tomatoes*; *Carol In A Thousand Cities*; *Coffee Will Make You Black*; *Last Exit To Brooklyn*; *The True Story of a Drunken Woman*; *Beautiful Swimmers, Learned Pigs and Fireproof Women*; and an all-time favorite, *She*.

Has anybody read *She*? "She who must be obeyed!" The book is by H. Rider Haggard, who also wrote a more famous book—*King Solomon's Mines*. Imagine the brash inspiration to title your book just—SHE. (Henry Miller loved Rider Haggard, by the way.) Now you tell me. Is that not good? And if it is, *why is it?*

A lot of writers don't take their titles as seriously as they should. Yes, *many* do, but I can tell you from experience teaching writing at an MFA in writing program, many do not. They will go with the first title that comes to mind. Or, with the second. They don't devote the time and effort required to produce a good title, because, I think, they don't see it as crucial. Further, their thought process behind selecting a title is often haphazard, or disorganized. It's not focused. It's not *directed*. They don't have a strategy, or a sense of purpose. This seems to me one of the biggest problems. That is, writers don't establish a set of goals for finding their title. The fact is, the title should represent the heart and soul of your book, story, or essay. Finding it isn't always easy, but it's well worth it.

The tradition of giving of titles in Western literature really came into its own with the novel. Titles existed before that, certainly, but it really wasn't until the novel emerged that titles took on a major importance of their own. For discussion's sake, let's say that tradition begins with

Don Quixote. You'll find disagreement here, but the novel as we know it wasn't around in a significant way before Cervantes took up his pen. (I'm referring to Western Literature, so this would exclude the much earlier *Tale of Genji* from Japan.) In any case, it is what comes after that that we need to examine. And examine we should. Tradition is the foundation upon which we build our own originality.

The novels that followed, the ones we know so well and have read and enjoyed, drew their titles from three basic sources.

One, the authors named their books after their main characters. In this category, we have many familiar books: *David Copperfield*; *Tom Jones*; *Robinson Crusoe*; *Moll Flanders*; *Jane Eyre*; *Henry Esmond*; *Oliver Twist*; *Silas Marner*; *Huckleberry Finn*; *Tom Sawyer*; and so on. It continued into the twentieth century with books such as *Martin Eden* by Jack London; *Sister Carrie* and *Jennie Gerhardt* by Theodore Dreiser; *Lucy Gayheart* by Willa Cather; and, as recently as 1963, John O'Hara's *Elizabeth Appleton.* Oddly, this major tradition has largely disappeared from contemporary fiction. I wonder why? Couldn't *The Catcher in the Rye* have been titled *Holden Caulfield*? Couldn't *Light in August* have been called *Joe Christmas*? If not, why not?

I don't think anyone would have a problem naming three or four novels from the eighteenth or nineteenth century that are named after their main characters. Can you name three or four others from the twentieth century—particularly after 1950—or the twenty-first? Of the top of my head, I can think of only a few: *Kate Vaiden* by Reynolds Price; *Elizabeth Costello* by J.M. Coetzee; *I Am Charlotte Simmons* by Tom Wolfe; and, recently, Roddy Doyle—who gave us the irresistibly titled *Paddy Clarke Ha Ha Ha*—published a novel titled *Paula Spencer.* Maybe this will signal a comeback for the eponymous novel. I suppose we can include *Franny & Zooey* as first names and *Mr. Bridge* and *Mrs. Bridge*, as last.

This tradition, by the way, obviously extends to other countries and languages. Think of *Anna Karenina*; *Nana*; *Eugenie Grandet*; *Thérèse Raquin;* and *Madame Bovary.*

There are subcategories within this first general category that actually have very strong traditions, as well. Or maybe they might be better called different species within the same genus. In any case, there is a tradition of naming books after *places.* Think of *Wuthering Heights*; *Barchester Towers*; and, easing nicely into the twentieth century, *Winesburg, Ohio*; *Tobacco Road*; *Cannery Row*; and the once-infamous *Peyton Place.* There are books named after songs, namely, *The Grapes of*

Wrath and *Bright Lights, Big City.* There are books and stories named after weather systems, "Rain;" *Typhoon*; and *The Perfect Storm.* Death has inspired quite a few authors, and undoubtedly will continue to do so: *Death Comes to the Archbishop*; *Death of a Salesman*; *Death of a Hornet*; "The Death of the Moth;" *Death in Venice*; and *The Death of Ivan Ilyich.* Phone numbers have even been called upon: *Butterfield 8* and *Dial M for Murder.* You could take this down some mighty strange roads. But the point is that authors will—and should—do anything and everything to find the best title for their book. And if it's lurking on your telephone receiver, so be it.

The second major category for naming novels is naming them with quotations from other, outside sources. The two deepest wells from which authors have drawn are the Bible and Shakespeare. But it's not limited to just them.

The Bible has supplied, and continues to supply, authors with great material for book titles. Think of *The Sun Also Rises*; *East of Eden*; *Lilies of the Field*; *Vile Bodies;* and two plays, *The Little Foxes* and *Inherit the Wind.* Shakespeare has provided authors with a treasure trove of material. *The Sound and the Fury* is probably the most famous Shakespeare-inspired title. We have *The Dogs of War; Pale Fire; Brave New World; The Winter of Our Discontent; Ape and Essence; The Bubble Reputation*; and, in the 1940s, *To Be or Not to Be*, which was a movie, and a comedy at that. John Updike titled a story of his, "I am Dying, Egypt," which is from *Anthony and Cleopatra.* Let's not forget *Remembrance of Things Past.* But, wait, that's not even a correct translation of Proust's title, *À la recherche du temps perdu.* I guess it's actually the translator's—C. K. Scott Moncrieff's—title by way of Shakespeare.

Writers have drawn on other literary sources, of course. Fitzgerald got *Tender is the Night* from Keats. Think of *For Whom the Bell Tolls*, for example, which Hemingway took from John Donne. William Styron's *Darkness Visible* from Milton and *Lie Down in Darkness* from Thomas Browne. (Styron has a darkness theme going here.) J.D. Salinger went to Sappho, the Greek poet, for *Raise High the Roofbeam, Carpenters.* John O'Hara lifted *A Rage to Live* from Pope. Evelyn Waugh found *A Handful of Dust* in T. S. Eliot's "The Waste Land."

The third major tradition, and the one we are now within more so than any of the others, is titles *made up* by the author—original titles that come from no place else other than the writer's mind. The title may be something uniquely used on the cover—and not within the main text of the book. Or the author may draw from his or her *own* words and slap them on the cover. Again, think of Salinger's *The Catcher in the Rye.*

The state of titles today? Decide for yourself. How many titles can you roll off the tip of your tongue, titles that have stayed with you? I think of a few favorites: *Me Talk Pretty One Day*; *A Heartbreaking Work of Staggering Genius*; *Disgrace*; and *The Human Stain.*

Now, here is the *New York Times* fiction bestseller list for the week of September 10, 2007, beginning at the top: *A Thousand Splendid Suns*; *The Wheel of Darkness*; *Dark Possession, The Elves of Cintra*; *Play Dirty*; *The Quickie*; *Lord John and the Brotherhood of the Blade*; *Away*; *Sweet Revenge*; *Power Play*; *The Sanctuary*; *Loving Frank*; *Sandworms of Dune*; and *The Secret Servant.*

Which of these titles, do you think, will be immortal? If so, why? If not, why not?

Now, you may say, I'm not interested in those first two traditions. They belong to the past. I'm not going to take the nineteenth-century route and name my book after a *person.* How *quaint!* And I say—*why not*? Why shouldn't you title your book with the name of your main character? You forget that no one knew who David Copperfield was when Dickens put the name on the cover. It was someone's name—a character's name—that's all. Say you had a book titled *Steve Stannerson.* I just made it up. Not very good, I know. But the first thing I would ask myself when I see this on a book cover is *who the heck is Steve Stannerson?* Maybe I'll open the book and find out.

Then your title has done its job—or at least part of its job. I think it's patently clear that Reynolds Price was drawing upon that older tradition when he titled his book *Kate Vaiden.* By doing so, he immediately gave his book an aura of a *journey* and of a large struggle, both of which were normally attached to fat, eponymous novels of the past. And why shouldn't you search for a title from the Bible or from Shakespeare's works? I know that if I ever wrote a book, or an essay, on suicide, my title would be: *The Undiscovered Country.* Those are words spoken by the most famous near-suicide in history, Hamlet, and I don't think I could do any better on my own.

What makes a good title, then? I think for a title to be good it has to fulfill two main tasks. First, it has to be memorable. Easier said than done. Second, it has to be true to the essence, to the soul, of the book. A title can't possibly capture every emotion or action in a book, but it should, I think, at least represent some main artery, pulsing with blood, that flows through the book. If it doesn't, it's a kind of betrayal.

Here, I disagree with Nance Van Winckel. About what the title should be, she writes, "Although few creative writing textbooks offer aspiring writers much advice on titles, one I perused suggested that a poet try to find a title which would sum up what the poem was about. Please consider that a giant X has been drawn through this last sentence. I would rather aspiring writers get no advice at all on titles than this advice!" However, you can't escape this, nor should you. In fact, in the very next paragraph, Van Winckel writes about her own search, "During the time I'm on the hunt for the perfect title, I know certain operations are taking place. I am mulling over—and often on a subconscious rather than conscious level—what the poem or story is about. This seems to be part of directing those antennae."

I want to make clear that the purpose of this essay is not to refute Van Winckel's words. Her essay is absolutely wonderful, extremely learned, diverting, and helpful, and I highly recommend it. Her writing, as I said, is mainly about poets and poetry, though. From her, you'll get a good taste of the titles of Wallace Stevens, who sometimes, at least from his titles, seems more like a carnival barker or a Delphic Oracle than the sober, erudite, philosophical poet he is. (For me, it's telling that no one I know has ever quoted Wallace Stevens to me, as one would quote, say, Yeats, Frost, or Eliot. The *titles* are quoted, yes.) Speaking of poets, this reminds me of another of my favorite titles, Allan Ginsberg's *Howl*. I can't think of a better one. Forty-five years after the poem's publication, that one great from-the-gut title still has all its strength and unchained energy. Where did that come from, one wonders? How fascinating it would have been to have looked over Ginsberg's shoulder as he went through the process of naming this poem. Van Winckel also brings in titles of paintings, which is helpful.

So, let's take *She*. Is it memorable? God, I would hope so. Rider Haggard uses a pronoun to stand for a proper noun, and uses one that everyone has used thousands of times. This is same principle behind naming a movie *Them*—a real title of a real movie. *She* is also short—three letters, one syllable. And it shoots out of the mouth like a snake's forked tongue. Does *She* represent one of the main great pulses in the book? Well, once you read the book, you know that it does. All the drama, all the force, all the strange mystery of the title is more than compensated for in the woman who has lived for 3,000 years.

And, indeed, *Learned Pigs and Fireproof Women* in fact *is* about learned pigs and fireproof women. It's a history of carnival life through the ages, about hoaxes and con men. The learned porker in question is the nineteenth or eighteenth century—I forget which now—Toby, the Sapient Pig. Toby was foisted unto the British public as a pig who could not only think, but read and write. In fact, he wrote his autobiography, which the author Ricky Jay quotes and I have to say is quite good, for a pig.

Let's return to *The Sound and the Fury* and to *Macbeth*. Here is the source for Faulkner's title, spoken by Macbeth himself:

> To-morrow, and to-morrow, and to-morrow,
> Creeps in this petty pace from day to day,
> To the last syllable of recorded time;
> And all our yesterdays have lighted fools
> The way to dusty death. Out, out, brief candle!
> Life's but a walking shadow, a poor player,
> That struts and frets his hour upon the stage,
> And then is heard no more. It is a tale
> Told by an idiot, full of sound and fury,
> Signifying nothing.

What do you notice about the quote and the Faulkner title? They aren't precisely the same. Faulkner added the article "the" twice where Shakespeare does not have it. Is that ok? Sure, it's ok. Does anyone think Faulkner is trying to deny he took the title from Shakespeare? Of course not. He just knew, taken out of context, the words would do better with two "the's" when it became a title, standing alone. Consider it perfectly acceptable if you throw in an article or two to make a quotation work for you.

Robert Frost went to this same passage for the title of his poem of a boy being mangled by a buzzsaw, "Out, Out—".

What's also important about titles taken from quotations is that the context be relevant to the story to which the title is affixed. *The Sound and the Fury* is indeed, at least in part, "a tale told by an idiot"—he is Benjy. *East of Eden* is another example. The title comes from Genesis. It refers to Cain who, as we all know, slew his brother, Abel. Rebuked by God, Cain "went out from the presence of the Lord, and dwelt in the land of Nod, on the east of Eden." Steinbeck's book largely deals with the strife between two brothers, so the title takes on a profound, primal resonance, even majesty.

Now, as I mentioned, a trend in contemporary nonfiction titles is to attach a subtitle to the title. (Which, by the way, nineteenth-century novels employed regularly.) With a subtitle to straighten things out, you can have the freedom to be a bit arty, melodramatic even, or mysterious with your title. Here are a few, with their subtitles in parenthesis: *Into Thin Air* (*A Personal Account of the Mount Everest Disaster*); *The Perfect Storm* (*A True Story of Men Against The Sea*); *The Gutenberg Elegies* (*The Fate of Reading In An Electronic Age*); *Beautiful Swimmers* (*Watermen, Crabs and the Chesapeake Bay*); *Undaunted Courage* (*Meriweather Lewis, Thomas Jefferson and the Opening of the American West*). I would bet that not many of us remember a single one of these subtitles. If the book is good, and has a life, the subtitle eventually is cast off in the mind. Like the discarded first stage of a rocket, it drifts away forever, leaving just the main body of the missile. But when the book is first published, this helps the potential reader understand what the subject is, and makes the publisher and bookseller happy.

This is true of modern biographies, too. You don't just call a book, *The Life of Robert Moses.* You call it *The Power Broker.* You don't say you've written the biography of Winston Churchill. You say you've written *The Last Lion.* The subtitle and the picture on the cover will make things crystal clear, and you get to have your dramatic title. What these two titles do is to single out a particular facet or aspect of the person whose life has been written to create the image the biographer believes is essential. *The Last Lion.* Well, in three words we know William Manchester thinks Churchill is fearless, noble, terrifying and, in a way, beautiful. And there will never again be anyone like him.

A personal aside, if I may. I believe it's relevant to the subject at hand and may be helpful, and that is why I'm including it here. When I was trying to come up with a title for my own first book, I presented myself with three main goals. I didn't think it was right, or possible, to try for more. That, I reasoned, would simply weaken any title as it tried to satisfy more and more requirements, like a decision made by committee. The book is about living in a small village in the South of France and about having a vegetable garden there. The garden helped me connect to the villagers, and to the village, and to the land of Provence. What I told myself I should accomplish with my title was

1.   To let people know the book was about France.
2.   To give them some idea that it was about the land.
3.   That the title be brief, and strong.

And, it goes without saying, I wanted it to be unforgettable.

All the while I was trying to think up a title, I tried to keep the spirit, the soul, of my book within me, close at hand. I let that guide me. After three days of head scratching and mulling, I came up with two words: *French Dirt*. To me, those two words accomplished what it was I had set out to do. I stopped there.

My agent hated it. So did my editor. I was completely thrown off by this. My agent even went so far as to say, "My mother *hated* that title, and she's *never* wrong." They were so certain it was bad, that I began to have my doubts. To appease my editor, I tried to write other titles and showed her some I had discarded. She didn't like any of them, and neither did I. So, we temporarily dropped the matter. The title didn't have to be decided on right away, and so all of us, gratefully, put that issue aside. Some four months later, as the time neared for the manuscript to go to press, I reluctantly brought the title question up again.

"Uh, what about the title?" I asked my editor.

In her singy Southern voice she said, "Oh, hell, you might as well call it *French Dirt*. That's what everyone down here is calling it anyway!" What I hadn't realized was that as the manuscript circulated amongst the staff at my editor's office, the people who looked at it had to call it *something*. Since the only name it ever had was *French Dirt*, that's what they called it. I guess after a few months, it didn't sound that bad to my editor. "You have to give me a subtitle, though!" she ordered. "Otherwise, people will think it's an erotic novel, or some damn thing." And that's how the book ended up being titled *French Dirt: The Story of a Garden in the South of France*.

Finally, there's a whole category of titles whose main characteristic is that they are patently, dramatically, unabashedly direct, and obvious. I like these titles very much. They never assume literary airs. They also are incredibly democratic; they communicate their message to every single person in the planet, without exception. I'm referring to titles like, *How to Win Friends and Influence People*; *Everything You Wanted to Know About Sex But Were Afraid to Ask*; and, in a literary vein, a once-popular popular book used by some aspiring playwrights called *Write That Play!* (Notice that exclamation mark.) What's to be learned from these titles? The power of plain English. The power of directness. The power of simplicity. In a way, the titles of Emerson's essays are the archetype for this kind of title: "History;" "Love;" "Friendship;" "Intellect;" "Self-Reliance;" etc. We are grateful for his Yankee thrift and no-nonsense directness. Thoreau, too, was economical within *Walden*, as E. B. White noted, with chapter titles such as "Economy;" "Sounds;" "Solitude;" and "Visitors." We might take a lesson from these writers and reject the temptation to be artfully obscure or pyrotechnically brilliant with our title so as not to be accused of being a simpleton.

To wit: I found a wonderful title in Michael Ondaatje's book, *The English Patient*. It's mentioned in the "Acknowledgements" section, where the author credits a book called *Unexploded Bomb*. The two words handed to us in the form of a title carry with them the tension of a bomb that hasn't been diffused yet. Notice, too, it's not "The" *Unexploded Bomb*. That would make it particular to *one* bomb. What seems a somewhat ungraceful expression becomes an amazingly direct, memorable title that makes you slightly nervous. The author of *Unexploded Bomb* had the focus and the confidence to write exactly what the book is about without trying to make it "literary."

So, what can you do to put some memorable words on the cover?

I think there are several things you can do. The first thing I would strongly recommend is that you leave finding the title until after you've finished the book. I really think it's something that should be done in reflection, with the completed manuscript before you. That doesn't mean you can't have a working title. But books change as they're being written. Even if you know you're writing about the Great Fire of 1908, how can you be sure exactly what you've said about the fire until you've finished saying it?

Second, I would set aside a definite block of time uniquely devoted to thinking about your title. Only work on the title, nothing else. That way, you dignify the task. That way, you acknowledge its significance.

Third, I would scratch out on a piece of paper what it is you believe your book (or story or essay) is about, what it is you've discovered. This can be in the form of a paragraph or several sentences. Then, from there, it will be easier to distill, to boil it down to its essence.

Fourth, I wouldn't settle on the first, second or third title you come up with. Work at it. Revise. Put your efforts away for a day. Then look to see which of your efforts are, as Ezra Pound characterized art, "news that stays news." Remember, once it's on the cover, you can't take it off.

Fifth, be bold. Be dramatic. You may not have spent time in a mental hospital and so can't come up with *Girl, Interrupted*. But that shouldn't stop you from writing a great title. You've got your main characters. You've got Shakespeare. The Bible. Milton. John Donne. You've got your own imagination. That's a powerful arsenal.

8

The Eminent Domain of Punctuation

"There are some punctuations that are interesting and there are some punctuations that are not."

—*Gertrude Stein,* Lectures in America

"Are *you* kidding?!?"

This line, which I still find incredibly funny, is from Terry Southern's masterpiece, *The Magic Christian.* It's a wonderfully, joyfully, politically incorrect book. Thank God, Southern wrote his stuff before the "Commissars"—as Alan Cheuse calls them—could get to him with their pitchforks. Southern was a master, perhaps our greatest master, of the multiple exclamation mark and multiple question mark, as well as of italics. In fact, he was a black belt in punctuation, period, as it is used as a writing weapon. Others in this league are Mark Twain—well, he stands alone—and J.D. Salinger, and now David Sedaris—writers who use punctuation for more than its mere utilitarian purposes. They use it as one of the arrows in their writing arsenal, like nouns, verbs, adjectives.

Punctuation, while not precisely a major subject in the arena of writing, is, I think, a highly under-discussed and under-examined subject. (Well, perhaps used to be, what with *Eats, Shoots & Leaves.*) Especially with regard to how it can contribute to the style and content of a work. It is a wonderfully agile and resourceful tool, and goes far beyond simple grammar. And so, without further ado, here they are:

The question mark	?
The exclamation mark	!
The period	.
The comma	,
The semicolon	;

Quotation marks	" "
Parentheses	( )
Ellipses	....
The dash	—
The hyphen	-
Brackets	[ ]

And assorted minor players....

Each of these marks or symbols has its own personality, its own *character*. As Rimbaud spoke of the vowels in his poem of the same name, *Voyelles,* I think you could try to, as he said of them, "tell your latent birth." In fact, some poets have tried, notably Maurya Simon in her book, *A Brief History of Punctuation.* This is an excerpt, about the question mark:

I. The Creation of the Question Mark

It grew slowly, atom by atom, curving
its serpentine line around a doubt.
For eons it hung suspended in the air,
like a shepherd's crook, an ebony cane
a blind woman hung out at midnight
on an invisible clothesline.

It did not form itself from Adam's mouth,
it did not sprout as a kinky white hair
from Gilgamesh's never-trimmed beard,
it did not electrify loose ganglia
into synaptic fright in God's mind,
nor curdle the earthworm, nor shape
the sickle that mows down everything.

Like a lily, it roused itself to life,
unfurling into reason's limbo quietly,
and it left in its wake a single teardrop,
a tiny pin-prick of dew, a dab of salt
for the air minions to lick eternally—
that minute mirror begetting wonder.

We'll return to poetry and to writing about punctuation.

Punctuation, that spine of grammar, is drilled into us as relentlessly and as frequently as the parental, "Stand up straight!" During the first years when we begin writing, we forget periods; commas are a mystery;

and quotations marks are another galaxy, far, far away. The whole *idea* of punctuation is odd, when you think about it. That's because we learn language by speaking. Nobody taught us to say "period" at the end of a sentence. We just stopped. In other words, it's not natural to have these signs imposed upon us. It's a code we have to learn, and the learning of it takes time. Some of us never quite do learn it.

To hear what it would sound like to be taught punctuation by sound, we only have to turn to some old Hollywood movies. In the 1940s and 50s, when female assistants were still called secretaries and when they took dictation, it's not so unusual to come upon a scene in which a boss, in a boxy brown suit with his moustache and brilliantined hair, is dictating a letter. His body language says, "I'm important," and the secretary carefully notes his every word as if he were Lincoln. He might go on something like this:

> Dear Mr. Andrews *comma*. It is my sad duty to inform you that your client *comma* Mrs. J *period* Grenville Harthwell *comma* is dead *full stop* Here is a list of her effects *colon* Two sets of ivory chopsticks *semi colon* one silver trophy for second place in the Pinecrest Garden Club annual tulip extravaganza *comma* hybrids *semicolon* one lottery ticket for the Irish Sweepstakes *semicolon* and one *quotation mark* Win With Wilkie *close quotation mark* presidential pin *full stop* Yours very sincerely *comma* R *period* Ripley Fansworth *comma* Esquire *full stop*

But we are not taught this way. The fact is, punctuation is order imposed upon the chaos of the written word. There are established rules—obviously, or it couldn't be taught with any certainty—but it is not an exact science. Not everyone agrees with how or when a comma should be employed, for example. This is why publishing companies have their own style books. It's also why there are three or four major, big-selling and often contradictory Manuals of Style—Chicago, MLA, AP, etc. Grammar, and specifically punctuation, like any other subject we learn as a student, can seem unfair.

Poets often bend, twist, and cavort with punctuation in ways a prose writer simply couldn't. e. e. cummings comes to mind. (See how, even with his name, he makes a fool of capitalization?) cummings left periods and commas, and especially parentheses, floating in white space all by themselves, or itself, the effect of which is to slow you, the reader, down considerably, if not to a full stop. It also makes you see said punctuation mark as being as important as any of the words that dangle in air. Here's a brief example:

l(a

le
af
fa

ll

s)
one
l

iness

The champion of champions of the *dash* is Emily Dickinson:

> 'Twas love—not me—
> Oh punish—pray—
> The Real one died for Thee—
> Just Him—not me—

But poets have their own rules, and they are not always the rules of prose writers. So, with some reluctance, we must leave them now. In prose, the all-time dash champion has to be Laurence Sterne, the eighteenth-century English novelist who wrote *Tristram Shandy*. He employs the dash, or what might be called the superdash, almost as bizarrely as Louis-Ferdinand Céline does ellipses in his later works.

Like Miss Stein, I have my favorite punctuations and my not so favorites. But it's more a matter, I think, of trying to understand how these marks are employed and determining how they can be used in creative ways. These symbols are nearly hieroglyphic. The question mark **?** certainly would fit very neatly into any Egyptian hieroglyphic panel. (In fact, it's not too far from the hieroglyphic symbol for "u.") Brackets [ ] would, too. Where did these symbols come from? They seem so assured, so *right* for what they do. It almost seems as if they sprung full blown from the punctuational womb, or from Zeus' head, or thigh.

The question mark. Reading a sentence for the first time, sight reading, as it were, before you know it's a question, can cause you, once you see the familiar mark at the end, to intone upward to indicate the interrogative? (That's a trick, to prove a point.) Gertrude Stein would disagree with that. She said, "It is evident that if you ask a question you ask a question but anybody who can read at all knows when a question is a question as it is written in writing. Therefore I ask you therefore wherefore should one use it the question mark." Of course, she cheats by beginning that second sentence, the fulcrum of her argument, with, "I ask you." I think the point is that quite a few other writers have deemed it necessary to employ the question mark, and it doesn't seem to have caused mass confusion.

In Spanish, they take no chances. When a sentence is a question, the Spanish tell you right from the beginning, placing a question mark, upside down (not to compete with its concluding partner) right at the start. So, "How are you?" in Spanish would be: "¿Como está usted?" No confusion there. They do the same thing with an exclamation. "I love you!" would be: "¡Te amo!" I have no idea how that got started, or if other languages do anything like that. I remember learning Spanish as a kid and thinking, How strange.

Referring back to the Terry Southern example, you can see how the question mark, or multiple question marks, can make you laugh. It's perhaps odd and maybe impossible to analyze, but in some cases the more question marks you add, the funnier the idea is. Beginning with one,

> Late?
Then two,
> Late??
Then three,
> Late???

I have no idea why two is funnier than one and three even funnier. Southern uses multiple questions mark, sometimes separated by an exclamation mark, throughout *The Magic Christian*. He learned from a master, William Burroughs, one of the very few writers who made him laugh. They worked together at one point to try to turn Burroughs' most celebrated book, *Naked Lunch,* into a screenplay. (The book was later made into a movie, but not using the Southern/Burroughs script.) So, Southern knew Burroughs'—or, as some style books would have it, Burroughs's—work well. And what he saw in *Naked Lunch* was italics (another Southern favorite), ellipses and multiple question marks and multiple exclamation marks used to great comedic effect. At one point, Doctor Schafer, "the Lobotomy Kid," one of Burroughs' many mad doctors, feels betrayed,

Schafer wrings his hands sobbing: "Clarence!! How can you do this to me?? Ingrates!! Every one of them ingrates!!"
The Conferents start back muttering in dismay:
"I'm afraid Schafer has gone a bit too far…."
"Brilliant chap Schafer…but…"
"Man will do anything for publicity…."

The exclamation mark has great potential for comedic effect, as you can see. No one knows this better than David Sedaris. He takes it to the limit in his story, "Season's Greetings to Our Friends and Family!!!" This is from his book, *Holidays on Ice*. It's in the form of one of those Christmas letters we all have gotten from a family, usually written by the mother, summing up what went on in the Jones (or whatever) family this past year. In this case, it's the Dunbar family, and a lot has gone on. This is how it begins,

Many of you, our friends and family, are probably taken aback by this, our annual holiday newsletter. You've read of our recent tragedy in the newspapers and were no doubt thinking that, what with all their sudden legal woes and "hassles," the Dunbar clan might just stick their heads in the sand and avoid this upcoming holiday season altogether!!
You're saying, "There's no way the Dunbar family can grieve their terrible loss *and* carry on the traditions of the season. No family is *that* strong," you're thinking to yourselves.
Well, think again!!!!!!!!!!!!

Yes, *twelve* exclamation marks. And I have a feeling Sedaris played around with this before coming up with the number that would reveal this woman's character the best and set the stage for this bizarre story. More exclamation marks to follow in this story, I assure you. Sedaris also makes hay with question marks in this essay in the great Burroughs/Southern tradition. The letter tells the story of a hysterically perky housewife who finds herself host to her husband's daughter, Khe Sahn, the product of a liaison during his stint in Vietnam years ago and unbeknownst to all until now. The whole essay is a delight of over-emphasis. As the coiled Mrs. Dunbar writes in her letter,

"Out of nowhere this land mine knocks upon our door and we are expected to recognize her as our child!!!!????????"

There are funny exclamation marks and funny questions marks throughout.
I'm pretty certain that Nick Hornby read *The Magic Christian,* because he acts very Terry Southern-like at one point in his book about reading, *Housekeeping vs. The Dirt,* published in 2006. He's writing about Bob

Dylan's book, *Chronicles,* telling us that when he heard Dylan was publishing a book about his life, he "found it hard to imagine what it would look like. Would it have a corny title—*My Back Pages,* say, or *Times, They Have A-Changed*? Would it have photos with captions written by the author? You know the sort of thing: 'The eyeliner years. What was *that* all about?!!?'"

Yes, punctuation is funny.

Let it be stated here, in its own paragraph, that Tom Wolfe has received the Lifetime Achievement Award for the Creative Use of Italics, Dashes and Assorted Original Uses of Punctuation to help create his singular style.

You could write pages about the comma and about the period. But first I want to talk a bit about brackets. [ ] I love brackets. I love them on the one hand because of their shape. For some reason, speaking of marks that indicate some sort of an aside, I'm more attracted to this shape than to the shape of the parenthesis ( ). (By the way, one of the most original and effecting uses of parentheses is, I think, in the form a book title: *In Parenthesis* by David Jones, which is an account of his time as a soldier in World War I. A life in parenthesis.) I doubt I can explain why, and I'm sure it's utterly personal. I like them more because they formally allow personal interventions. Parentheses do, too, but I feel with brackets I'm more comfortably able to make a comment on the goings on in the essay—much like someone commenting on a film to a partner in a theater, supplying a piece of information, without which, the friend would miss something that, while not necessarily critical, would certainly mean he or she would go without a small, delicious pleasure.

Samuel Johnson had negative feelings about parentheses, and they revolved around the matter of clarity. He felt they were interruptive. "Johnson's attention to precision and clearness in expression was very remarkable," Boswell writes. "He disapproved of a parenthesis; and I believe in all his voluminous writings, not half a dozen of them will be found." I have twice that many in this essay alone. So much for clarity.

I'm not a big fan of the semicolon. I think of it as the hermaphrodite of punctuation. It's both a period and a comma, with neither the personality nor the passion of either. It even looks like a hermaphrodite, with both organs, as it were. And when it is used, it generally has a tentativeness to it that seems to me to indicate it doesn't know which part of itself to emphasize. So often a period, or a comma, would be better to use than a semicolon. I think one of its only consistently legitimate uses is in a series of lists in which commas and conjunctions are seriously involved. There, they can save the reader from confusion. Otherwise, I leave it in storage.

But now we come to the big boys. As Gertrude Stein put it,

> So now to come to the real question of punctuation, periods, commas, colons, semi-colons and capitals and small letters.
> I have had a long and complicated life with all these.

As indeed anyone who has tried to be a writer has, too.

Stein's entire essay is fascinating and worth reading. She has thought about punctuation profoundly, albeit from her own particular vision, and this vision she sees as *the* vision. Here's what she has to say about the period:

> When I first began writing, I felt that writing should go on, I still do feel that it should go on but when I first began writing I was completely possessed by the necessity that writing should go on and if writing should go on what had colons and semi-colons to do with it, what had commas to do with it, what had periods to do with it.... Inevitably no matter how completely I had to have writing go on, physically one had to again and again stop sometime and if one had to again and again stop some time then periods had to exist.

Gertrude Stein may have come around about periods—"Beside[sic] I had always liked the look of periods and I liked what they did."—but she never did about commas. She didn't like them. She said that "commas are servile and they have no life of their own, and their use is not a use, it is a way of replacing one's own interest.... A comma by helping you along holding your coat for you and putting on your shoes keeps you from living your life as actively as you should lead it and to me for many years...the use of them was positively degrading."

Did you know that punctuation could be so personal?

Indeed, it seems to be. Paul Robinson, a professor at Stanford University, published a highly opinionated essay in the *New Republic* twenty-five years ago titled, "The Philosophy of Punctuation." It begins winningly, "Punctuation absorbs more of my thought than seems healthy for a man who pretends to be well adjusted." Robinson states categorically that the period and the comma "are the only lovely marks of punctuation...because they are simple." Well, he also readily confesses to being "anal," as he puts it, so perhaps "neat" might be a more appropriate word than "simple" to describe the comma and the period. In any case, I don't agree with his aesthetics. I think the question mark is lovely, although I think it also possesses other qualities as well. It embodies gracefully three disparate typographical elements: the circle—in this case, half a circle—the straight line, and the period. I love its shape. Robinson admits he keeps a "neat house," and so perhaps the question mark seems unlovely to him because it's *not* neat. It's open-ended, incomplete, unfinished. And curvy. (Robinson might be pleased to read that Gertrude Stein said of exclamation marks, "They are ugly.") But this is all a matter of opinion, and I find it somewhat amazing that I'm writing about the loveliness of punctuation in the first place.

I enjoyed reading Robinson's essay—which is mainly a cry for the proper use of punctuation, and what he deems that to be—because he cares. He has strong, sincere feelings about, and for, punctuation. He understands each of these symbols has a *character.* (I see he's not a fan of the semicolon, either.) But when he says, "Good punctuation, we feel, makes for clean thought," I pause. I think it's the other way around. That seems to me the more interesting statement. And I fervently disagree with him on "the use of italics for emphasis," as he describes it. He says, "Italics rarely fail to insult the reader's intelligence. More often than not they tell us to emphasize a word or phrase that we would emphasize automatically in any natural reading of the sentence." This is definitely not true *in comedy.* Look at J.D. Salinger. Here's a bit from *The Catcher in the Rye.* Holden is talking to a girl named Sally and proposes that they run away together. She declines, and offers this logic, "'In the first place, we're both practically *chil*dren. And did you ever stop to think what you'd do if you *didn't* get a job when your money ran out. We'd *starve* to death. The whole thing's so fant*as*tic....'"

Look at Terry Southern. ("Are *you* kidding?!?")

Look at Mark Twain! The grandfather of all American writers, as Faulkner declared. His use of punctuation is probably, overall, the most masterful of any American writer who has ever lived. You could go to school on his use of the comma alone, for example. But we are talking of italics. One small example from *Huckleberry Finn.* The king and the duke have just given one of their theatrical salads to a group of townspeople who live along the Mississippi. It appears the performance was too brief:

"Twenty people sings out:

"'What, is it over? Is that *all*?'"

In the case of comedy, the reader would often most definitely *not* emphasize the italicized words naturally.

Actually, I believe you have to have a sense of humor when you write about punctuation. It's an inherently funny subject. Just look at the title of this essay. How in God's name did a series of punctuation marks, more or less randomly put down, come to mean *swearing?* I do have concern about the right use of punctuation, but I'm far more interested in the way certain writers use punctuation creatively. In how they use it as part of their writing arsenal.

James Joyce—who has probably been dragged into more literary brawls than he would care to recall—made what may be the most memorable use of the period in the history of the English language—by eliminating it. This occurs at the end of *Finnegans Wake.* (By the way, Joyce scholars, why no apostrophe in "Finnegans"?) These are the last lines of the book: "Take. Bussoftlhee, mememormee! Till thousendsthee. Lps. The keys to. Given! A way a lone a last a loved a long the" Yes, there is no period. Which leads us right back to the start of the book: "long the riverrun, past Eve and Adam's, from swerve of shore to bend of bay, brings us by a commodius vicus of recirculation back to Howth Castle and Environs." So, it's Finnegan beginagain. Which means, I suppose, that you'll be reading this book forever.

So expectant are we, so accustomed to the presence of the period that its absence is almost, or was almost, inconceivable. You end a sentence, you place a period. You end a book, you clearly place a period after the last sentence. Not Joyce.

A period is not just "simple" as Robinson describes it. It's also strong, undeniable. I love its simplicity, but I'm in *awe* of its strength. Its force. You can't deny a period. You can't rebel, or overthrow its authority. Try. Try. Try. See? You can't. The period is It. Who. Must. Be. Obeyed. Nothing comes close to having that Authority in punctuation. Not the comma, which, if you like, eventually, as these things go, can, by its repetition and, apparent unstinting use, be ignored, or at least overridden, or have its authority diminished. Attempt to diminish the authority of the period. Good luck. Even the question mark hasn't that same authority. What do I mean? I mean, even a question mark can be disobeyed. It says to you: raise your eyebrows at the end of the sentence. And you reply, Maybe I will, maybe I won't. Or maybe not as high as you would like. A period says, Stop. And you stop.

Not only that, but the period plays a major role in the creation of a sentence for writers. That is, in deciding how a sentence will look, and what it will say. With the period, you know you will have made a complete sentence, you will have a clear, definitive, unmistakable *end.* I hate Jim. Think of that without a period. I hate Jim It's a floating entity. I mean to say that a writer forming a thought will think of that thought in terms of a sentence—that is, in terms of a unit with a definitive beginning and end, and so part of his or her creative process, creative deliberation, is based on that simple fact (among others, of course). They are thinking within boundaries.

Joyce is a good transition when it comes to quotation marks. Much could be written about quotation marks, but I'll just comment on a small subculture—their gradual elimination. I'm not sure where it started, but in *A Portrait of the Artist as a Young Man,* published in 1916, James Joyce replaced the traditional quotations mark with a dash. This practice he continued in *Ulysses.* The singular is correct here, because Joyce put a dash at the beginning of the sentence instead of a quotation mark but understood that a second dash was not needed as a conclusion. It was easily inferred. His former employee, Samuel Beckett, perhaps sensing an opening here, eliminated quotation marks, dashes, and everything else but the period when he had his characters speak in his 1953 novel, *Watt.* Though not a widespread practice, this total quotational nudity has been followed by some authors who are writing today, notably Tim O'Brien in his 1990 novel, *The Things They Carried.* The novelist Cormac McCarthy eschews quotation marks, as well. I'm not sure what the benefit is to the reader here, other than the simple idea of: Hey, we may not need these things. It would seem that the question is: At what point does all this stripping down start to make things unclear and unnecessarily difficult for the reader?

Just a few words about ellipses. They indicate something that has been left out. The dictionary definition is: "a. The omission of a word or phrase necessary for a complete syntactical construction but not necessary for understanding. b. An example of such omission. A mark or series of marks (. . . or * * * , for example) used in writing or printing to indicate an omission, especially of letters or words." Their use is pretty unexciting, almost legal in feeling. But not always. Like any other punctuation mark, it can surprise you. It can be used by a gifted, daring writer in a way that takes it to another level, to where it becomes a new color for his or her palette. This is the case with Jean Rhys's use of ellipses in her novel, *Good Morning, Midnight,* in a passage we referred to earlier. (The title is from an Emily Dickinson poem, by the way.) But now we can examine it more closely in terms of what she's doing artistically with ellipses.

We come upon the narrator in a sad state. She's hit bottom in Paris. She has no money, or friends. She has a complete lack of self-esteem, of *amour propre*. She's a wreck, in short. She's having a drink after dinner, all by herself. And here Rhys makes ellipses absolutely mystical. Their use is unique. They say a huge amount about the narrator's life and her state of mind:

> I stayed there, staring at myself in the glass. What do I want to cry about? … On the contrary, it's when I am quite sane like this, when I have had a couple of extra drinks and am quite sane, that I realize how lucky I am. Saved, rescued, fished up, half-drowned, out of the deep, dark river, dry clothes, hair shampooed and set. Nobody would know I had ever been in it. Except, of course, that there always remains something. Yes, there always remains something….Never mind, here I am, sane and dry, with my place to hide in. What more do I want? … I'm a bit of an automaton, but sane, surely – dry, cold and sane. Now I have forgotten about dark streets, dark rivers, the pain, the struggle and the drowning…. Mind you, I'm not talking about the struggle when you are strong and a good swimmer and there are willing and eager friends on the bank waiting to pull you out at the first sign of distress. I mean the real thing.

This is *not* nonfiction, to remind you. This is not a case where we look to ellipses to inform us that some part of the text is unnecessary for us to grasp an argument. In fact, the ellipses here do not refer to *any* prose that we know of that has been eliminated. They refer—to what? To drunken or emotional pauses the narrator is literally making? To psychic gasps of breath? Or are they a kind of sad, forlorn rhythm of a wasted life? Or are they tears? Whatever they are exactly, they communicate a sensation of desperation, of barely hanging on. How Rhys came upon that possibility for the use of ellipses, I don't know, but I would say it's inspired. It's poetry.

Authors with as diverse literary backgrounds and times as Edith Wharton and John Rechy have used ellipses for creative, stylistic purposes, far beyond their basic yeoman's job. Add the aforementioned William Burroughs and Louis-Ferdinand Céline to that company as well. I'm sure you can find plenty of others.

Good writers will use anything and everything to tell their story. For some, more than others, that means that odd typographical crew that we employ every day, dutifully, perhaps even resentfully, page after page.

9

It's About Nothing: Finding Subjects for Creative Writing in Everyday Life

The story goes that the nineteenth-century French short story writer Guy de Maupassant once claimed that he could write a story about anything. A companion took him up on that and challenged him to write a story about a piece of string. What could be more banal, more uninspiring than a piece of string as a subject? The result? "The Piece of String," by de Maupassant, a now classic short story by the French master.

De Maupassant was showing off, but the story does have relevance to you and to your writing. Because there will come a day when you might find nothing to write about, and you will despair. The first few works you have in you probably will spill out like a dam burst. That doesn't mean writing them will be easy; it just means that you will know what you want to write about—more or less—and the struggle you have with it has to do more with craft. So, you write your memoir. You write your novel. So you write four or five personal essays or stories on subjects that have always enthralled you. So you write the profiles of three or four people you admire. What next? You're presumably in this for the long haul. Well, if you don't have a problem finding subjects, God bless you. All I can say is that writers I know often struggle finding subjects, particularly if they've been at it for a while. Sometimes to the point that they are in despair and think, well, I just don't have *anything* to say. I'm done. I'm finished. The well's run dry.

What *are* you going to do if the well runs dry? Where will you find your inspiration? Well, maybe you'll be lucky like the nature writer Robert Finch. His subjects come to *him*. A small, most interesting and unusual bat flies down his chimney and into his study—the very same study where he is sitting and trying to write. A subject for a Robert Finch essay, "A Visigoth in the Study"! Another day, a hornet gets stuck behind his windowpane and vainly tries to get out. In the very same study where he's trying to write. *Another* subject for a Robert Finch essay. In fact, it's called, "Death of a Hornet," which is in fact the title of the book from which those two essays are taken. What will fly down his chimney next, one wonders, and present itself to Finch as he idly searches for a subject? I am tempted to write him to see if he would consider renting out his studio to me on off hours. I'll just sit there and wait to see what tumbles down the chimney or flies through the window, then write about it.

But the point is this. Other people sitting in that same chair where Finch sits could have the same bat fly down the chimney and the same hornet fly against the windowpane and it would do nothing for them. It wouldn't inspire them at all. Oh, perhaps they might be curious about this little bat, and maybe attempt to free it and maybe tell their friends about it. But would they write an entire essay about it? And even more unlikely, would they write an entire essay about a *hornet*? Well, Finch did, for two reasons, I suspect. One is: it's clear he loves these kinds of things. He responds to them. He genuinely likes to write about them. The second reason is that, and you can tell this by the writing, Finch is obviously a very curious fellow. Passionately curious. He needs to find out everything he can about this little bat and this fierce insect. That leads him to many fascinating places, and gives the writing substance and allure. We, the readers, are charmed and delighted by his infectious curiosity.

But the most important thing to observe here is that Robert Finch is absolutely unafraid to write about something as "insignificant" as a hornet. In fact, he's confident that it's significant enough to warrant writing about. Why? Because he trusts his own predilections and lets them go where they will lead him. And here we turn to Emerson, one of our great wise men, to give this idea some big-name clout. In his famous essay, "Self-Reliance," Emerson writes, "To believe your own thought, to believe that what is true for you in your private heart is true for all men—that is genius." When in doubt, turn to Ralph Waldo Emerson.

The fact is that some of your deepest, most fervent passions can show themselves in little things, in ordinary matters. This, I think, is especially true if these things have a tradition to them, a history, if they are among the "old verities," as I heard one writer say, describing putting her wash out to dry on the line and watching the wind billow the clothes. Speaking of domestic chores, there is a wonderful description of housecleaning in *Walden*:

Housework was a pleasant pastime. When my floor was dirty, I rose early and, setting all my furniture out of doors on the grass, bed and bedstead making but one budget, dashed water on the floor, and sprinkled white sand from the pond on it, and then with a broom scrubbed it clean and white; and by the time the villagers had broken their fast the morning sun had dried my house sufficiently to allow me to move in again, and my meditations were almost uninterrupted. It was pleasant to see my whole household effects out on the grass, making a little pile like a gypsy's pack, and my three-legged table, from which I did not remove the books and pen and ink, standing amid the pines and hickories. They seemed glad to get out themselves, and as if unwilling to be brought in.

Thoreau on sweeping up. Literature.

By the way, Robert Finch isn't alone in his fascination with vespids. Others have been inspired by stinging bugs. Seeing wasps in the snow led Loren Eiseley to ruminate about life, and especially about death, and to write the essay, "The Brown Wasps." Finch is also obviously drawing on—or harkening to—Virginia Woolf's essay, "The Death of the Moth." In Finch's case, a spider seizes the hornet and dispatches it. In Woolf's case, the moth in her window is trying to escape but cannot and wearies itself unto death. Woolf wrote that "this gigantic effort on the part of an insignificant little moth against a power of such magnitude [i.e., death] to retain what no one else valued or desired to keep, moved one strangely." This ordinary incident, which we all have witnessed countless times, provoked Woolf to speculating about the unknowable. And then to write.

Now, I don't mean to suggest you should run out and write about, say, caterpillars, or mice. But if they fascinate you and you want to write about them, by all means. I know a woman who wrote an entire book about earthworms. It's called *The Earth Moved: On the Remarkable Achievements of Earthworms.* She received good critical response, too. No, the lesson here is not that you should write about things that weigh less than a pound, but that you should follow your passions, wherever they take you. The point is, you should *want* to write about these bugs or whatever. That's something you need to be aware of in daily life. These passions are often engaged in just a fleeting moment. The trick is to be aware of your eagerness and curiosity and to respond to it. You have to allow yourself to *see.*

Despite the fact that W.H. Auden declared that he did not know "of anyone in the United States today who writes better prose," M.F.K. Fisher still had to answer to those who felt that she was just a "food writer." This seems absurd, but it's true. Here's what she said: "There is a communion of more than our bodies when bread is broken and wine is drunk. And that is my answer, when people ask me: Why do you write about hunger, and not wars or love." This was far before the time when a writer might sit down and write about the ecstasies of peanut butter and have readers recognize it as literature. M.F.K. Fisher dared to write about food—its pleasures and subtleties—at a time when that seemed odd. The result? *The Art of Eating*, an American literary masterpiece.

I believe in the importance of the inspiration of other genres of art. So, I want to turn to the great American painter Edward Hopper. No one that I know of took daily life and turned it into the most breathtaking art more memorably than he did. I would suppose the most famous painting of his is *The Night Hawks*, that study of light and loneliness in an all-night diner. You also may remember his portraits of people in hotel rooms, of people sitting disconsolately on beds, of people staring vacantly from chairs on porches. Hopper also frequently painted the facades of ordinary buildings in ordinary towns. He seems almost deliberately *not* to have chosen dramatic events as his subjects. Just look at the titles of his paintings: *Drug Store*; *Gas*; *Railroad Train*; *August in the City*; *Summertime*; *Hotel Lobby*; *Barber Shop*; *East Side Interior*; *Hotel Room*. There is not a "Raft of the Medusa" or a "Judith Beheading Holofernes" in his work.

These subjects suited his dedication to, and fascination with, light and form. He painted the light of dusk, of early morning, of night, and, most difficult, of mid-day. Again, some titles: *Seven A.M.*; *Early Sunday Morning*; *Morning in a City*; *High Noon*; *Cape Cod Afternoon*; *House at Dusk*; *Night Shadows*. He seemed to have given himself the task of painting the light of every hour in a day, and may, in fact, have done just that. And what a love affair he had with lines and angles, with the geometry of shapes!

Now, one of the first things you notice here, it seems to me, is that the subjects are very ordinary. People in a diner late at night. A woman usher taking a break in a theatre. A woman seated by herself having a cup of tea or coffee. A couple in their apartment building, seated, the man reading the paper. A man at a gas pump. An empty street in the early morning. A woman seated on her front porch. Yet, would anybody here deny that any of these paintings are art? And extremely fine art, at that—even some of the finest art ever produced by an American painter? Moody, reflective, mysterious, measured, lonely—yes, lonely—but painted so gloriously, with such a grasp of color and of composition. They also seem to reach us very deep within, to a place where all of us are a bit lonely, and a little afraid, and very human. They celebrate life through their beauty, and yet they point out the fragility of it, too. All through the mundane.

But you may say: *Edward Hopper is a painter!* It really doesn't matter what he chooses to paint. He's only concerned about composition and color. Not me. I'm a writer. I have to *say* something about these people, this damn gas station you've thrown in my face. I can't just put them on the page and expect people to jump up and down and say that's brilliant writing.

Well, the point is that Hopper was drawn to these subjects because it was through them that he could best express his beliefs and his art. It was certain aspects of these subjects that inspired him to greatness. He saw things in them. Or he allowed himself to see things in them that inspired him to paint them. Maybe he fell in love with the strange harsh lighting of the late night diner. Who knows? Well, the point is, he allowed himself to envision that as worthy of a painting, worthy of his highest efforts and hardest labor.

Ok, you'd like an example from a writer? Let's turn to Pablo Neruda, the great Chilean poet. In 1954, he published a book called *Odas Elementales*, "Elemental Odes," which is about common things in life. I'm very happy to see that these odes have been issued in a book of their own in English, called *Odes to Common Things*. You can also find many of these odes in any anthology of Neruda's work. Neruda's odes have titles like, "Ode to a Fallen Chestnut," "Ode to the Tomato," Ode to the Clothes." Others subjects include books, bird watching, even laziness. These are not arch poems of the intellect. These are passionate, believing poems expressing gratitude and wonder. Let me quote again just a few delectable lines from "Ode to the Clothes." You can't get much more basic in your subject matter than a pair of pants, now can you?

> Every morning you wait,
> clothes, over a chair,
> for my vanity,
> my love,
> my hope, my body
> to fill you,
> I have scarcely
> left sleep,
> I say goodbye to the water
> and enter your sleeves,
> my legs look for
> the hollow of your legs,

and thus embraced
by your unwearying fidelity
I go out to tread the fodder,
I move into poetry,

I want to emphasize here again that this chapter is not necessarily about urging you to write about button-down shirts or flip-flops. Although, again, if they inspire you, go to it. I think flips-flops are a terrific subject for a poem, actually. It's about allowing yourself to feel sympathy, passion, and tenderness toward our little lives and how they are led.

All right, you say. Pablo Neruda's a *poet*. Poets can write about anything. They're supposed to get all dewy-eyed over lockets their dead wife left behind and leaves falling off trees and even clothes. Forget the fancy-dancy poetry. Give me some meat and potatoes. Give me some prose.

Let's turn to E. B. White. All roads of nonfiction and, actually, fiction (remember *Charlotte's Web*) eventually pass by his doorway, even if only fleetingly, at one time or another. Now, I don't know how many of you have read White, or how many of you are fans, but whatever the situation, I recommend you read his essay, "Here Is New York." Written over fifty years ago, it's still the best thing ever written about New York. But that's not the essay I want to refer to. This essay of White's is about—a pig. No, not about that famous pig, Wilbur, that appears in *Charlotte's Web*, but a real pig that lived on White's farm in Maine. The essay is called "Death of a Pig."

It's a simple story, really. White had a pig. The pig got sick. White didn't know what was wrong with him. He called the vet. The vet came and treated the pig. Nevertheless, the pig died. That's it. That's the story. No plot, other than that. And just a few characters, one of them being White's dachshund, Fred. Yet. Yet! Let me quote a small selection, somewhat ridiculous, but that's the point. White has given the sick pig some castor oil to cure him, and that has not worked. He has been advised to give the pig an enema, which he does:

> I discovered, though, that once having given a pig an enema there is no turning back, no chance of resuming one of life's more stereotyped roles. The pig's lot and mine were inextricably bound now, as though the rubber tube were the silver cord. From then until the time of his death I held the pig steadily in the bowl of my mind; the task of trying to deliver him from his misery became a strong obsession.

Each time I read this essay, and I have read it many times, I find myself a bit weak in the knees at the end. The compassion of it!

All right, you say. E. B. White lived on a farm. He had all those animals to inspire him. I don't live on a farm! I live in a house in suburbia! The only pig we ever see is Porky. My cat is useless. I need an example that's relevant to my life.

Ok, I'll give you one: by Robert Benchley.

In case you don't know Benchley, he was a sweet, self-effacing man who frequented the Algonquin Round Table in New York in the 1930s and 40s and had a small but wonderful career in the movies. I highly recommend his short film, *The Sex Life of the Polyp*. (Yes, *The Sex Life of the Polyp*.) Among the things Benchley wrote were theater criticism and essays. One of the most delightful of these essays is called, "My Face." (You can find it in Phillip Lopate's *The Art of the Personal Essay*.) Now, I ask you, is that not something you have, too? A face? I'll wager you do. Look what he does with his own visage:

> Some mornings, if I look in the mirror soon enough after getting out of bed…I turn quickly to look behind me, convinced that a stranger has spent the night with me and is peering over my shoulder in a sinister fashion, merely to frighten me. On such occasions, the shock of finding that I am actually the possessor of the face in the mirror is sufficient to send me scurrying back to bed, completely unnerved.

There you were, every day, looking into the mirror, not realizing there was a subject for a delightful little essay.

One final example that gives new meaning to the word "ordinary."

I give you Nicholson Baker and his book, *Double Fold: Libraries and the Assault on Paper*. It's a book that grew out of an essay he wrote about the disappearance of—ready for this?—card catalogs in libraries. Read the book if you don't think anyone could be passionate about such a thing. Or write more than a hundred words about them. Now, consider this. Suppose you went to your inner self, or to some friends who are already a bit skeptical about this career of yours as a writer, and you informed them you were going to write an essay, maybe even a book, about the *disappearance of card catalogues*. (Let's imagine Baker's book doesn't exist.) And not only that, you were passionate—angry and outraged—about the disappearance of card catalogues. You were going to write your heart out about—card catalogues. Hmmm, nods you inner self. Oh, boy, say your friends. I hope his—or her—parents don't find out about this. Such a shame all that money they spent on a college education.

Now, this is the moment you, as a creative writer, have to be acutely aware of, I think. Because it's right at this moment when your inner self, or inner whatever, is liable to say: Who cares about card catalogues—especially with Iraq, AIDS, terrorism, global warming…I mean what is with you? But the point is: you do. You know and believe it *is* something to write an essay or even a book about. So, this is what I mean about daily life. These moments. I can't say they will come to you all day, every day. I can't say every strong feeling you have will be worthy of writing about. Some things just don't accommodate themselves to lengthy discourse. But I can tell you something for certain. You'll never know if you turn away from those moments, in which your authentic self reacts, the light goes on, the heart responds, the passions fire. As Marianne Moore said, "The thing is to see the vision and not deny it; to care and admit that we do."

So, if you find yourself looking at, say, the pencil in your hand and marveling at how such a simple instrument has changed the world in so many ways, why, you just may want to write about it. And you should.

It's got at least as much going for it as a piece of string.

10

Maxims about Writing

A maxim, as defined by the *Random House Unabridged Dictionary*, is "an expression of a general truth or principle." The form and spirit of this section is based on the famous book of maxims by La Rochefoucauld, the seventeenth-century French nobleman. La Rochefoucauld's maxims cover a wide area of moral territory. Each maxim is a world unto itself, and his book can be read from any point whatsoever. These maxims cover a multitude of aspects of writing, from simple how-to suggestions to trying to find the courage to write to the feel of the pencil on a page. One maxim, one thought. They are easily assimilated—hopefully—taken in small doses. The reader can read casually, flipping through until something catches his or her eye. Ideally, there should be something to satisfy whatever mood the writer is in, or whatever need or curiosity he or she has at that moment. The principle is to isolate a general truth about writing and to dramatize it. These are words to help boost a writer.

* * *

Reading, for a writer, is a practical matter. How do you know what can be done unless you've seen it done by others?

Good writing is like the transfer of impulses via the synapses of the brain. There should be a leap between writer and reader, like the electrical leap that bridges the gap between synapses. The completion of the writer's message is made by the reader's imagination and passion.

Keep a good dictionary next to you. Employ it often to track down the best word with the vigilance of a bounty hunter.

Distance = Clarity^2. Give yourself a day between the editing and rewriting. For clarity like the light in the South of France, give yourself two weeks.

If you have a motto as a writer, it might be, "In my heart I trust."

If you have a thought, an idea, a change, don't *ever* delay putting it down—not even for three seconds. It will escape forever. No amount of pleading, prayer, or cursing will bring it back. A small part of your mind will be like the Flying Dutchman, searching fruitlessly for the lost thought for all eternity.

There is no good or bad subject, no inherently dull or interesting subject. The subject is not that critical. The *passion* is. Proof: read *Beautiful Swimmers*, a book about crabbing that won the Pulitzer Prize.

Consider a writing group. *Anything* to help legitimize your quest, and to assuage your loneliness and paranoia.

Attend a reading. It's important to see the word made flesh.

Don't judge yourself as a writer. You have plenty of relatives, friends, and acquaintances to do that for you.

Try not to think of your work published. That greedy dream will eat up everything in its path, including your penchant for truth.

Warm up before you begin to write. Hemingway sharpened pencils with a knife. Understand that you'll be cold at first, like a car engine. It takes a while to get the machinery going, to be at full throttle.

If you want consistently striking examples of the use of a specific word towards a desired effect, look to the humorists. There, a whole paragraph can turn on a single word.

Don't be afraid of outright enthusiasm. Remember William Blake: "Exuberance is Beauty." Do you need a more righteous authority?

Bad grammar will expose you as an incompetent writer as blatantly as cutting in line will expose you as a deceitful person.

A person who criticizes other writing thoughtfully will tend to write that way.

Ask yourself after you've written something: Do I want to claim proud ownership of this? Or do I want to disown it? Will I, like Peter when asked if he knew Jesus, deny ever having known this man—deny this piece of writing?

If you find a book you love, don't hoard the discovery. Reading is not a contest.

"I write to make sense of my life," John Cheever said. So, a normal part of the writing experience is to be in a state of ignorance.

Most anything you do in writing can be improved.

Before you settle on a word, look it up. Make sure of its definition. See what its synonyms are. Look them up. Is there a better word lurking in a shadowy corner somewhere?

Read Flaubert's letters and step into the mind of a man gripped at the throat by writing.

Do you think writing should be easier than it is? Why? Why should it be easy to write a sentence that will thrill people today, and twenty years from today?

When you are writing, when you are in it, the work is not just mental, it's *physical*. Hemingway used to grunt like a warthog when he was in the thick of it. Flaubert had what he called his "Shouting Room." Give way to those groans, cries, and shouts.

Write some of whatever you're writing in longhand. Sculpt the words with your ink or lead. Experience the connection between your mind and your pen or pencil. You are an artificer as well as an artist.

Revision *is* writing.

"We learn how to write when we react vigorously to what we have written, discovering in the process that we are able to improve our own writing or to feel satisfied with what we have written." –Paulo Freire. The second part of that equation—to feel satisfied with what we have written—is the most difficult to assume, and the most satisfying.

You do not see the chips and dust and hack marks on Michelangelo's *Pietá*, but you know they were there. Look at gorgeous sentences in the same way.

You want to find your voice? Listen: "Originality is in any case a by-product of sincerity."—Marianne Moore.

What is the *truth* of your past? "A memoir is how one remembers one's own life."—Gore Vidal.

Can't I change things in memoir? Can't I mix fiction and fact? "Tampering with the truth," writes Judith Barrington, "will lead you to writing a bit too carefully—which in turn will rob your style of the ease that goes with honesty."

Getting at a subject indirectly is often the most powerful way of approaching it. Gertrude Stein said something to the effect that "you get to know the Seine best by not looking at it."

Stop writing where you know what's going to happen next. The next day when you begin again, you'll have a place to go. That's what Hemingway did.

Flaubert said that what is a writer but a triple thinker? What did he mean by that? He meant, I think, that you are first the artist, the creator. You are second the critic who steps back and examines the writing with a cold clear eye. You are third the characters on the page with their thoughts and emotions—and, eventually, their independence.

Much of writing is purely mechanical, like wiring a house. Skill is often what's needed, not genius or talent.

What is the difference between *quick* and *fast*? A question like that should mean the world to you.

Think of this. If you write ½ page a day for 365 days, you'll have 182 pages—an impressive stack—in front of you.

The heart of all storytelling is character.

The most memorable, most efficient way to create character on the page is through dialogue.

How can we make a distinction between fact and truth in writing? We must, as Hemingway said: "A writer's job is to tell the truth. His standard of fidelity to the truth should be so high that his invention, out of his experience, should produce a truer account than anything factual can be. For facts can be observed badly, but when a good writer is creating something, he has time and scope to make it of an absolute truth."

Imagination is a muscle. If you haven't used it often, it's flabby, like any untested muscle. You have to get it in shape. That takes discipline. It's like going to the gym—just as painful, and ultimately, just as rewarding.

You can do a lot worse than take to heart what Hemingway has to say about writing. Writing meant everything to him. He worshiped it, and what he has to say rings with sincerity, acumen, and truth.

Only rarely has landscape or nature come close to haunting the mind like a character. In Turgenev, for example. But where else?

Sometimes you get lost. Completely. You feel as if you've been abandoned by every instinct, every skill, every bit of experience. It's as if you fell overboard a ship, and no one knew. Treading water, you watch helplessly as the ship slowly moves off into the distance, getting smaller and smaller, still smaller, then disappears. You're alone. Nothing around but empty sea. There is only one thing you can do. Have faith. Have *blind faith.*

Clarity in writing always returns to passion. Marianne Moore said it well: "When emotion is strong enough, the words are unambiguous."

Try cutting out the first paragraph of your story or memoir, or whatever you're working on. Just as an exercise. Pretty surprising, isn't it? And pretty humbling.

When you cut out something from your work, it doesn't disappear. An energy stays. The leaving-out provides a force all its own. The pruning

channels the creative sap to the prose that remains. Cutting is not delet-
ing then, it's adding.

You can get sick of any character you write about, and will.

Read the Brothers Grimm. They're more Freudian than Freud. They
have incomparable insight about deep secrets inside, about our most
murderous desires, plus a transporting imagination to bring us the relief
that we are not alone.

The road is long. We are discouraged often. When that happens, find
solace in this poem by C.P. Cavafy, the great twentieth-century Greek
poet from Alexandria:

The First Step

The young poet Evmenis
complained one day to Theocritus:
"I've been writing for two years now
and I've composed only one idyll.
It's my single completed work.
I see, sadly, that the ladder
of Poetry is tall, extremely tall;
and from this first step I'm standing on now
I'll never climb any higher."
Theocritus retorted: "Words like that
are improper, blasphemous.
Just to be on the first step
should make you happy and proud.
To have reached this point is no small achievement:
what you've done already is a wonderful thing.
Even this first step
is a long way above the ordinary world.
To stand on this step
you must be in your own right
a member of the city of ideas.
And it's a hard, unusual thing
to be enrolled as a citizen of that city.
Its councils are full of Legislators
no charlatan can fool.
To have reached this point is no small achievement:
what you've done already is a wonderful thing."

If you think you're the only one who has been repeatedly humbled by writing, read this section from "Burnt Norton," one of T.S. Eliot's *Four Quartets*:

> Words strain,
> Crack and sometimes break, under the burden,
> Under the tension, slip, slide, perish,
> Decay with imprecision, will not stay in place,
> Will not stay still.

And, from "East Coker":

> That was a way of putting it—not very satisfactory:
> A periphrastic study in worn-out poetical fashion,
> Leaving one still with the intolerable wrestle
> With words and meanings.

In order to write well, you need to focus, and you cannot focus unless you have fiercely guarded writing time.

You can take something from every good writer. One useful thing is enough. You shouldn't expect more than that, even from the best.

Don't feel odd or discouraged because you don't like or understand a certain author—particularly if the author is renowned. It could be the wrong time for you to be reading this author: It could be too early. Or it simply could be that you'll never like this author. So what? Do you like all *places?* Can't you tolerate the fact that someone loves glaciers, and Germany, and you don't? Is that any reflection on your acumen, on your sensitivity, on your values?

What to write? A character—Buddy, I think—in one of J. D. Salinger's books says, "Think of the story you'd most like to read. Then go out and write it yourself."

You have to throw everything you have into your writing. Literally. Balzac, who certainly did that, said it well: "If the artist does not throw himself into his work like…a soldier against a fortress without counting the cost; and if, once within the breach, he does not labor like a miner buried under a fallen roof; if, in short, he contemplates the difficulties instead of conquering them, one by one…then the work remains unfinished, it perishes, is lost within the workshop, where production becomes impossible, and the artist is a looker-on at his talent's suicide."

Be brave. (Easier said than done.)

Read only five or six maxims at one time. After that, the element of surprise is lost.

Your heart will guide you, not your brain. "The mind cannot for long play the role of the heart," said La Rochefoucauld.

Stay loyal to the writers you love. Don't disavow them because of cultural fashions or the latest politics. Don't deny your love and enthusiasm. That's the first step to denying your passions about your own work.

Good prose is not only like music, it *is* music. It has a pace, rhythm, cadence, even a melody. It may not be as evident as a tune by Mozart, but it's there. Part of the pleasure in reading a passage by Conrad or Proust or even Hemingway is musical. You can almost picture yourself humming the words.

Some things others have said better. Sometimes it's best to stand back and let them speak:

"How simultaneously enfeebling and insulting is an empty page! —William Styron, *Sophie's Choice*

"O the thousand appliances one needs for writing even a sentence!"—Virginia Woolf, *Diary, v. I*

"One has to go into the most remote corners of a subject in order to discover the simplest things."—Marguerite Yourcenar, *Memoirs of Hadrian*

"And besides, I like its name [Siberia], like Borneo, Abyssinia, and Labrador, without knowing exactly why. This power of syllables will seem a waste of time to many, but it is rare that poetry does not uncover earthly powers."—François Mitterrand, *The Wheat and the Chaff*

"Trash is the inevitable result whenever a person tries to do for himself or for others by the writing of poetry what can only be done in some other way, by action, or study, or prayer."—W.H. Auden, "Tennyson"

The quiet, cool early morning; the open notebook; the simple pen—all these forever, and still hold great significance and appeal. How much more can you reduce your life, your work? How much more can you essentialize it?

If you can't see what's next, trust your heart. As the Yiddish proverb has it, "The heart is half a prophet." This is what Philip Roth placed at the beginning of his first book, at the beginning of his career.

Marianne Moore said it right—again. What you need to produce good writing is humility, concentration, and gusto.

A writer can take almost any criticism about his or her work except if you say it's boring. Then he or she wants to jump off a bridge.

No critic who ever lived will cause you as much doubt or anguish about your writing as yourself.

Never hesitate. Put it down. *Now. This instant.*

When you go to stay at someone's home, don't take any books with you. Hungry for a read, you'll encounter books you've never read. The potential for disappointment is there, true, when you go this route, but so is the element of discovery and wonder.

Writing will never abandon you. As long as your mind is lucid and you can push a pen or pencil across the page, writing will be there for you. It's constant—unlike almost any other profession or calling you can think of.

Read *The Unquiet Grave* by Cyril Connolly for lovely maxims.

Creeds and stances will go in and out of fashion. It may take longer in the universities, because those with power have tenure. Even they are eventually deposed, however. But "the human heart in conflict with itself," as Faulkner described our condition, is not subject to politics. Remember that in the maelstrom. That's your subject.

Pablo Neruda, the great Chilean poet, knew about fear:

Fear

Everyone is after me to jump through hoops,
whoop it up, play football,
rush about, even go swimming and flying.
Fair enough.

Everyone is after me to take it easy.
They all make doctor's appointments for me,
eyeing me in that quizzical way.
What is going on?

Everyone is after me to take a trip,
to come in, to leave, not to travel,
to die and, alternatively, not to die.
It does not matter.

Everyone is spotting oddnesses
in my innards, suddenly shocked
by radio-awful diagrams.
I do not agree.

Everyone is picking at my poetry
with their relentless knives and forks,
trying, no doubt, to find a fly.
I am afraid.

I am afraid of the whole world,
afraid of cold water, afraid of death.
I am as all mortals are,
unable to be patient.

And so, in these brief, passing days,
I shall not take them into account.
I shall open up and closet myself
with my most treacherous enemy,

Pablo Neruda.

Memorize a passage of poetry or prose that takes you. Get it inside your body.

Jealousy is unavoidable when you are a writer. There is always someone undeserving getting the prizes and the money. Just make sure jealousy is only an appetizer and not a main course.

Still stymied by lack of a subject? Look at Ruth Orkin's book of photographs, *A World Through My Window*. What beauty, just from her apartment window, that she allowed herself to see.

For a reading list, look to the books the authors you admire praise in their *own* novels or essays.

You should not try too hard to escape God or religion in your work. You don't have to believe to write fervently about belief.

Writers have an array of names to describe their first drafts: *vomit, puke, garbage, shit, trash, drivel, crap*. Well-known writers. Somehow, though, they seem to turn lead—or garbage—into gold.

Write every day if you can. Why should Sunday be any different than Thursday if you're a writer?

When you no longer have heroes, how can you make yourself one?

Remember the poet Theodore Roethke, "I learn by going where I have to go."

There *are* people who will understand and love your work. Not necessarily your mother and father. Probably not, in fact.

Sometimes your "failure" as a writer is simply due to not admitting to the real emotions you're feeling about the subject.

The last word to Marianne Moore: "The thing is to see the vision and not deny it; to care and admit that we do."

Notes

Introduction

P. 2, T. S. Eliot, "East Coker." In *The Complete Poems and Plays* (New York: Harcourt, Brace, 1971), V. 1-11.

P. 2, Billy Collins, "75 Needles in the Haystack of Poetry," *The Writer's Chronicle* (September 2006), 19.

P. 4, John Berryman, "A Strut for Roethke." In *77 Dream Songs* (New York: Farrar, Straus and Giroux, 1971), 20.

Chapter 1

P. 7, Barry Lopez, *About This Life: Journeys on the Threshold of Memory* (New York: Alfred A. Knopf, 1998), 13.

P.7, Eudora Welty, *One Writer's Beginnings* (Cambridge, MA: Harvard University Press, 2003), 11.

P. 9, Richard Poirier and Mark Richardson, eds. *Robert Frost: Collected Poems, Prose, & Plays* (New York: Library of America, 1995), 853-54.

P. 9, William Strunk, Jr. and E. B. White, *The Elements of Style* (New York: Longman, 2000), 66-7.

Pp. 9-10 "An Interview with Susan Cheever," *The Writer's Chronicle* (May/Summer 2005), 43.

P. 10, Sarah Lyall, "Novelists Defend One of Their Own Against a Plagiarism Charge in Britain," *New York Times*, December 7, 2006.

P. 11, Mark Twain, *The Adventures of Tom Sawyer & The Adventures of Huckleberry Finn* (Ware, UK: Wordsworth Classics, 1992), 280.

Pp. 11-12, James M. Cain, *The Postman Always Rings Twice* (New York: Vintage, 1989), 3.

P. 12, William Faulkner, "Barn Burning," *Twelve American Writers* (New York: Macmillan, 1962), 751.

Pp. 12-13, James Crumley, *Dancing Bear* (New York: Vintage, 1983), 7.

P. 13, Marianne Moore, "Foreword," *A Marianne Moore Reader* (New York: Viking, 1974), xiii.

Pp. 13-14, Ernest Hemingway, *The Complete Short Stories of Ernest Hemingway* (New York: Charles Scribner's Sons, 1987), 302-3.

P. 14, Merrill D. Peterson, ed. *Thomas Jefferson: Writings* (New York: Library of America, 1984), 19.

P. 16, Robert Frost, 776.

P. 16, James Agee, "Knoxville: Summer of 1915," *The Best American Essays of the Century,* Joyce Carol Oates, ed. (Boston: Houghton Mifflin, 2000), 174.

P. 17, Robert Frost, 857.

Chapter 2

P. 19, Sven Birkerts, "Flaubert's Anatomy." *American Scholar* (Winter 2004), 138.

P. 19, Charles Carlut, *La Correspondence de Flaubert, étude et répetoire critique* (Paris: A.G. Nizet, 1968), 421. All translations, save for those from Steegmuller's book, are mine.

P. 20, Ibid., 415.

P. 20, Ibid., 421.

P. 20, Ibid., 421.

P. 20, *The Letters of Gustave Flaubert,* 1830-1857, Francis Steegmuller, trans. (Cambridge, MA: Harvard University Press, 1980), 83.

P. 20, Henry James, *Literary Criticism: Volume Two* (New York: Library of America, 1984), 315.

P. 20, Ernest Hemingway, *Selected Letters,* Carlos Baker, ed. (New York: Charles Scribner's Sons, 1981), 624.

P. 20, Ernest Hemingway, *A Moveable Feast* (New York: Collier Books, 1964), 134.

P. 20, Joan Didion, "Last Words," *New Yorker* 9 November 1998, 76.

P. 23, T. S. Eliot, "Johnson As Critic and Poet." In *On Poetry and Poets* (New York: Farrar, Straus & Cudahy, 1957), 195.

P. 23, Hemingway, *A Moveable Feast,* 126.

Pp. 23-24, Isak Dinesen [Karen Blixen], *Out of Africa* (London: The Folio Society, 1980), 198.

P. 24, Thomas Hardy, *The Return of the Native* (New York: New American Library, 1959), 75.

P. 25, Gilbert White, *The Natural History of Selborne* (London: Oxford University Press, 1974), 46.

P. 25, Marianne Moore, "Interview With Donald Hall," *A Marianne Moore Reader* (New York: Viking, 1974), 271.

P. 25, Ibid., 271.

P. 26, John Cheever, *Falconer* (New York: Alfred A. Knopf, 1977), 119.

P. 26, Truman Capote, *Breakfast at Tiffany's* (New York: Random House, 1958), 87.

P. 27, Milan Kundera, *The Unbearable Lightness of Being* (New York: HarperPerennial, 1991), 20.

P. 28, *The Letters of Gustave Flaubert,* 158.

Chapter 3

P. 29, Milan Kundera, *The Unbearable Lightness of Being* (New York: HarperPerennial, 1991), 20.

P. 29, T. S. Eliot, "East Coker." In *The Complete Poems and Plays* (New York: Harcourt, Brace, 1971), V. 3-4.

P. 30, *Random House Unabridged Dictionary*, 2nd ed. (New York: Random House, 1993), s.v. "etymology."

P. 31, William E. Umbach, "Etymology." In *Webster's New World Dictionary of American English* (New York: Webster's New World, 1988), xxvi.

P. 31, *Random House Unabridged Dictionary*, 2nd ed., s.v. "hut."

P. 33, *Random House Unabridged Dictionary*, 2nd ed., s.v. "hysterical."

P. 34, *Random House Unabridged Dictionary*, 2nd ed., s.v. "holocaust."

P. 34, *Random House Unabridged Dictionary*, 2nd ed., s.v. "quell."

P. 35, *Random House Unabridged Dictionary*, 2nd ed., s.v. "odonate."

P. 35, *Random House Unabridged Dictionary*, 2nd ed., s.v. "entomology."

P. 35, Thomas Sappington, e-mail to author, November 30, 2006.

P. 36, Michael Tomasky, "The Phenomenon." *New York Review of Books* (30 November 2006), 14.

P. 36, Sven Birkerts, *The Gutenberg Elegies* (Boston: Faber and Faber, 1994), 95.

Pp. 36-37, Diana Wells, *One Hundred Birds and How They Got Their Names* (Chapel Hill, NC: Algonquin Books, 2001).

P. 37, "Walking." In *The Essays of Henry D. Thoreau* (New York: North Point Press, 2002), 149.

P. 37, Ibid., 149-50.

Chapter 4

P. 39, J. Corominas, *Diccionario Crítico Etimológico de la Lengua Castellana, v. 3* (Madrid: Gredos, 1954), 242.

P. 39, John Ayto, *Dictionary of Word Origins* (New York: Arcade, 1990), 89.

P. 39, Gregory Rabassa, *If This Be Treason: Translation and Its Dyscontents [sic]* (New York: New Directions, 2005), 19.

P. 40, Vladimir Nabokov, *Lectures on Literature* (New York: Harcourt Brace Jovanovich, 1980), 134.

P. 43, Rabassa, *If This Be Treason*, 6.

Pp. 43-44, Adam Jacot de Boinod, *The Meaning of Tingo and other Extraordinary Words from around the World* (London: Penguin, 2005), viii.

P. 44, Ibid, viii-ix.

P. 44, Ibid, viii.

P. 44, Ibid, ix.

P. 44, Ernest Hemingway, *The Old Man and the Sea* (New York: Charles Scribner's Sons, 2003), 17.

P. 45, Honoré de Balzac, *Cousin Bette* (Harmondsworth, UK: Penguin, 1984), 123.

P. 46, John Noble, "World's Languages Dying Off Rapidly." *New York Times*, September 17, 2007.

Chapter 5

P. 50, *Robert Frost: Collected Poems, Prose, & Plays* (New York: Library of America, 1995), 39-40.

P. 52, Seamus Heaney, *Crediting Poetry: The Nobel Lecture* (New York: Farrar, Straus, Giroux, 1995), 50.

P. 52, Ibid., 51.

P. 53, Philip Larkin, *Collected Poems,* ed. Anthony Thwaite (London: Faber and Faber, 2003), 100.

P. 55, Seamus Heaney, 54.

P. 55, Ibid, 20.

P. 56, W. H. Auden, *Forewords & Afterwords* (New York: Vintage, 1974), 336.

Pp. 56-57, Elizabeth Bishop, *The Complete Poems: 1927-1979* (New York: Farrar, Straus, Giroux, 1984), 131.

P. 58, Ibid., 84.

P. 59, Pablo Neruda, *Selected Poems* (Boston: Houghton Mifflin, 1990), 333.

P. 59, *The Complete Poems of Cavafy,* trans. Rae Dalven (San Diego: Harcourt, Brace, Jovanovich, 1976), 27.

Chapter 6

P. 63, Ernest Shackleton, *South: The Story of Shackleton's 1914-1917 Expedition* (London: W. Heinemann, 1938).

P. 63, Piers Paul Read, *Alive: The Story of the Andes Survivors* (Philadelphia: Lippincott, 1974).

P. 66, Vivian Gornick, *The Situation and the Story: The Art of Personal Narrative* (New York: Farrar, Straus and Giroux, 2001).

P. 66, F. Scott Fitzgerald, *The Great Gatsby* (Peterborough, Ontario: Broadview Editions, 2007), 49.

P. 67, J.D. Salinger, *The Catcher in the Rye* (Boston: Little, Brown, 1991), 63.

P. 68, Jean Rhys, *Good Morning, Midnight* (New York: Harper & Row, 1982), 10.

P. 68, Joseph Conrad, *Lord Jim* (Harmondsworth, UK: Penguin, 1979), 9.

P. 69, Fyodor Dostoyevsky, *Notes from Underground* (New York: New American Library, 1961), 120.

P. 73, John Knowles, *A Separate Peace* (New York: Dell, 1963), 5.

P. 73, James Gould Cozzens, *Guard of Honor* (New York: Harcourt, Brace, 1948), 3.

Pp. 74-75, Sherwood Anderson, *Winesburg, Ohio* (New York: W.W. Norton, 1966), 64.

P. 75, Truman Capote, *In Cold Blood: A True Account of a Multiple Murder and Its Consequences* (New York: Random House, 1965), 244.

P. 76, Arthur Conan Doyle, "The Hound of the Baskervilles" in *The Complete Sherlock Holmes*, v. 2 (Garden City, NY: Doubleday, 1930), 679.

Chapter 7

P. 77, Nance Van Winckel, "Staking the Claim of the Title" in *The Writer's Chronicle* (March/April 2004), 38.

P. 82, Ibid, 42.

Chapter 8

P. 87, Gertrude Stein, *Lectures in America* (New York: Random House, 1935), 214.

P. 87, Terry Southern, *The Magic Christian* (New York: Grove Press, 1960), 120.

P. 88, Maurya Simon, *A Brief History of Punctuation* (Winona, MN: Sutton Hoo Press, 2002).

P. 90, E. E. Cummings, *Complete Poems* (New York: Liveright, 1991), 673.

P. 90, Emily Dickinson, "394" in *Twelve American Writers* (New York: Macmillan, 1962), 621.

P. 91, Gertrude Stein, 214-15.

P. 92, William S. Burroughs, *Naked Lunch* (New York: Grove Press, 1990), 94.

P. 92, David Sedaris, *Holidays On Ice* (Boston: Little, Brown, 1997), 45.

P. 92, Ibid., 49.

P. 93, Nick Hornby, *Housekeeping Vs. The Dirt* (San Francisco: Believer Books, 2006), 23.

P. 93, James Boswell, *The Life of Samuel Johnson* (New York: Random House, [nd]), 1034.

P. 94, Gertrude Stein, 216.

P. 94, Ibid., 217.

P. 94, Ibid., 219-220.

P. 94, Paul Robinson, "The Philosophy of Punctuation" in *The New Republic* (April 26, 1980), 28.

P. 94, Ibid., 29.

P. 95, Ibid., 28.

P. 95, Ibid., 30.

P. 95, J. D. Salinger, *The Catcher in the Rye* (Boston: Little, Brown, 1991), 132.

P. 95, Mark Twain, *Huckleberry Finn* (Ware, Hertfordshire, UK: Wordsworth Editions, 2001), 283.

P. 96, James Joyce, *Finnegans Wake* (New York: Viking, 1947), 628.

P. 98, Jean Rhys, *Good Morning, Midnight* (New York: Harper & Row, 1982), 10.

Chapter 9

P. 100, Robert Finch, *Death of a Hornet and Other Cape Cod Essays* (Washington, DC: Counterpoint, 2000).

P. 100, Ralph Waldo Emerson, "Self-Reliance" in *Essays: First Series* (New York: John W. Lovell, n.d.), 43.

P. 101, Henry David Thoreau, *Walden* (New York: Walter J. Black, 1942), 137.

P. 101, Virginia Woolf, "The Death of the Moth" in *The Art of the Personal Essay*, ed. Phillip Lopate (New York: Anchor Books, 1995), 267.

P. 101, W. H. Auden, "The Kitchen of Life" in *Forewords & Afterwords* (New York: Vintage, 1974), 485.

Pp. 101-2, M. F. K. Fisher, *The Art of Eating* (Cleveland: The World Publishing Company, 1954), vii.

Pp. 103-4, Pablo Neruda, "Ode to the Clothes" in *Selected Poems* (Boston: Houghton Mifflin, 1990), 333.

P. 104, E. B. White, "Death of a Pig" in *Essays of E. B. White* (New York: Harper & Row, 1977), 21.

P. 105, Robert Benchley, "My Face" in *The Art of the Personal Essay*, ed. Phillip Lopate (New York: Anchor Books, 1995), 511.

P. 106, Marianne Moore, "Humility, Concentration, and Gusto," in *A Marianne Moore Reader* (New York: Viking, 1961), 130.

Chapter 10

P. 109, Susan Cheever, *Home Before Dark* (Boston: Houghton Mifflin, 1984), back flap.

P. 109, Paulo Freire, *Letters to Cristina* (London: Routledge, 1996), 2.

P. 110, Marianne Moore, *A Marianne Moore Reader* (New York: Viking, 1974), 271.

P. 110, Judith Barrington, *Writing the Memoir* (Portland, OR: The Eighth Mountain Press, 1997), 28.

P. 111, Ernest Hemingway, "Introduction," in *Men at War,* ed. Ernest Hemingway (New York: Crown, 1942), xv.

P. 111, Marianne Moore, 271.

P. 112, C. P. Cavafy, *The Complete Poems of Cavafy* (New York: Harvest, 1976), 6.

P. 113, T. S. Eliot, *The Complete Poems and Plays* (New York: Harcourt, Brace, 1971), 121.

P. 113, Ibid., 125.

Pp. 113-114, Honoré de Balzac, *Cousin Bette* (Harmondsworth, Middlesex, UK: Penguin, 1984), 215-6.

P. 114, La Rochefoucauld, François, *Maxims* (South Bend, Indiana: St. Augustine's Press, 2001), 22.

P. 114, William Styron, *Sophie's Choice* (New York: Random House, 1979), 35.

P. 114, *The Diary of Virginia Woolf,* v. 1, ed. Anne Olivier Bell (New York: Harvest, 1978), 297.

P. 114, Marguerite Yourcenar, *Memoirs of Hadrian* (New York: Farrar, Straus, 1963), 338.

Pp. 114-115, François Mitterrand, *The Wheat and the Chaff* (New York: Seaver Books, 1982), 20.

P. 115, W. H. Auden, "Tennyson" in *Forewords & Afterwords* (New York: Vintage, 1974), 225.

P. 116, Pablo Neruda, "Fear" in *Selected Poems* (Boston: Houghton Mifflin, 1990), 358.

P. 117, Theodore Roethke, "The Waking" in *The Collected Poems of Theodore Roethke* (Garden City, NY: Anchor Books, 1975), 104.

P. 117, Marianne Moore, 130.

Name Index

Title Index